Adorable

ANIMAL
→QUILTING

Adorable ANIMAL QUILTING

20+ Charming Patterns for Paper-Pieced Dogs, Cats, Turtles, Monkeys and More

INGRID ALTENEDER

creator of Joe, June and Mae

PAGE STREET
PUBLISHING CO.

PAGE STREET
PUBLISHING CO.

First published in 2020 by
Page Street Publishing Co.
27 Congress Street, Suite 105
Salem, MA 01970
www.pagestreetpublishing.com

Distributed by Macmillan, sales in Canada by The Canadian Manda Group.

24   23   22   21   20   1   2   3   4   5

ISBN-13: 978-1-64567-058-2
ISBN-10: 1-64567-058-9

Library of Congress Control Number: 2019951642

Cover and book design by Laura Benton for Page Street Publishing Co.
Photography by Jonas Alteneder

Printed and bound in China

Dedication

FOR MY CHILDREN—
JONAS, SOPHIE AND EVA

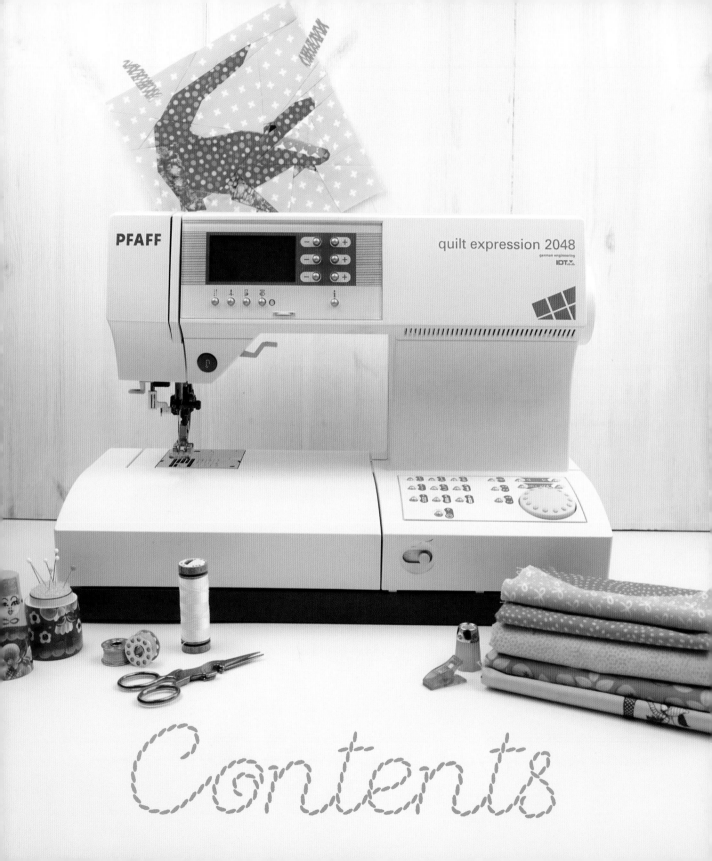

Contents

Introduction

Welcome to my quilting world of adorable paper-pieced animals.

Foundation paper piecing is a patchwork technique that allows you to create pictures with small pieces of fabric. It lets you sew those small pieces easily and accurately while being quite simple at the same time. It may seem daunting at first, but once you grasp the general concept, it's actually really fun, relaxing and may prove to be addictive. And, for me, another favorite part of paper piecing quilt blocks is speed. You can create some stunning handmade pieces without having to invest the time in sewing an entire quilt.

Paper-pieced quilt block patterns are perfect for wall hangings, table runners, mug rugs, pillowcases, bags, framed art and so much more. These cute blocks give you ample opportunity to be creative and turn them into something very special and personal.

Working in the fashion industry for most of my adult life has greatly expanded my love for yarn and fabric. I'm not a minimalist and was always drawn to rich colors and designs. Being exposed to a deeply rooted quilting community in North America while living there for a long time let me quickly evolve from simple shapes, such as squares and triangles, to more detailed blocks, such as the paper-pieced animals in this book. Experiencing these fascinating animals on my many travels across the globe inspired me to combine these beautiful animals with my love for quilting, resulting in these colorful animal quilt blocks for you to sew up in your favorite fabrics.

Don't be shy in your color combinations. . . . Go by the Iris Apfel quote: "More is more, less is a bore."

Animals are part of our lives, whether they're our friends and companions, our helpers or we simply find them fascinating.

A world without animals is likely a world we wouldn't want to live in. They are not only amazing but also a joy to look at, so they are the perfect choice for something as lasting as a quilt block.

I have included some easier blocks, such as Dominic the Dog (page 21) or the Baby Chick (page 30). These will be great to start your paper-piecing journey. If you are an experienced quilter, there are many blocks in this book that will inspire you to create tons of wonderful handmade items. I can assure you foundation paper piecing is not difficult or daunting; on the contrary, with the right tools, you will soon find it as much fun as I do.

So, get your sewing machine ready and let me introduce you to this fascinating technique.

QUILTING RULERS

LIGHTBOX

TAILOR'S CLAPPER

ROTARY CUTTER

CUTTING MAT

FABRIC GLUE PEN

PAPER

SCISSORS

TWEEZERS

THREAD

Tools and Supplies

As with any craft, a proper toolbox helps you immensely when working on your projects.

Paper piecing doesn't really require any fancy equipment, but a few tools will make your life a lot easier, so be sure to read this chapter and double-check whether there's anything essential that's missing from your toolbox.

THE BASICS

Sewing machine and sewing machine needles: Any standard sewing machine will work just fine for foundation paper piecing. I use size 80 sewing machine needles and change them often, since the paper dulls the needles fairly quickly.

Iron: An iron is essential when paper piecing; it gives you nice crisp seams and ensures a perfect quilt block. However, do not use steam, as it can distort your paper or fabric, or dissolve the printed pattern on your paper and leave stains on light-colored fabric!

Fabric: Foundation paper piecing is great for using smaller pieces of fabric. Many stores sell smaller pieces as "fat quarters"—this is a quarter of a yard of fabric, cut so it usually measures 18 x 22 inches (46 x 56 cm). A "fat eighth" would be half of a fat quarter. Depending on which way the fat quarter is cut in half, the fat eighth measures 9 x 22 inches (23 x 56 cm) or 11 x 18 inches (28 x 46 cm), but they aren't always available for sale in stores.

PAPER

A lot of specialty papers are available for foundation paper piecing, and it's easy to get lost or confused by all the variety. It's probably best to experiment with different papers to find out which you like best. I have worked with all sorts of papers and here's what I think:

Regular printer paper: At the moment, this is my paper choice. It's easy to use and cost effective; I use it in combination with a glue pen. And it is still thin enough to not be a headache when removing.

Freezer paper: This works great and is easy because you can just iron the fabric onto the paper and nothing slides off or moves, and obviously you don't need a glue pen. However, it's fairly thick and can get pretty bulky, especially when small pieces are involved. Because of its thickness, it's not as easy to remove afterward.

Foundation paper: It's wonderfully thin and perfect for tracing. It can also be used in your printer. Another advantage is that it's very easy to remove when finished. However, it can become quite costly if you do a lot of paper piecing. And it tends to curl if ironed.

OTHER SUPPLIES

Lightbox (optional): This tool is only necessary if you do a lot of fussy cutting. It lets you place your template perfectly on your fabric.

Rotary cutter and cutting mat: You really can't have too many if you're sewing and cutting a lot. Pictured on page 10 is a 12 x 12–inch (31 x 31–cm) rotating cutting mat. But I have large ones (23 x 34 inches [59 x 86 cm]) on every table in my sewing studio.

Good-quality craft scissors: There's really nothing worse than dull scissors. I use good-quality embroidery scissors for cutting small pieces of fabric and threads. Don't use fabric scissors for cutting paper, please; it dulls your scissors.

Fabric glue pen: Since I'm mostly working with regular paper, I use this pen all the time to glue the small pieces of fabric to the paper. I personally prefer using glue instead of pins. It also works fine with foundation paper.

Quilting rulers: There are tons of options out there. Those pictured on page 10 are the ones I use all the time. The ADD-A-QUARTER ruler, with a ¼-inch (6-mm) lip especially designed for paper piecing, gives you a perfect ¼-inch (6-mm) seam allowance. My 6 x 23–inch (15 x 59–cm) Omnigrid quilting ruler also comes with metric measurements.

Thread: Don't underestimate the importance of the quality of your thread. I use Aurifil 50-weight thread. It's thin but strong and made of 100 percent Egyptian Mako cotton. I only use white thread for my projects, since changing colors is virtually impossible with those little pieces, but cream or light gray are great options too, since they blend in nicely with most fabrics.

Tailor's clapper: This is probably one of my favorite tools. You just iron your sections quickly and then leave the clapper on. It keeps the heat of the iron in the fabric long enough to get nice flat seams.

Tweezers: These come in handy when removing the paper, especially from tiny corners.

Foundation Paper Piecing Made Easy

Before you get started, here are a few personal tips and comments:

The fabric consumption that I give with each pattern is on the generous side. Since foundation paper piecing is done on the reverse side of the pattern, it's easy to get confused with "mirrored thinking," especially in the beginning. So, it's better to have some extra fabric than to run out of fabric in the middle of sewing a block.

All of these patterns look fun with fabrics in realistic colors, whereby the animal is shown in the color it is in real life. But they are equally adorable with fantasy combinations, so let your imagination run wild. There are coloring pages for each pattern on my website www.joejuneandmae.de/coloring that can be downloaded for free with the code: animals.

PAPER PIECING STEP BY STEP

1. Photocopy or trace the pattern segments onto your choice of paper (I use regular printer paper, but see page 11 for more options and details).

   Cut out the segments along the dotted lines.

   Place the segments as they are on the numbered overview. (I like doing that, just so I know where everything goes.) Referring to the numbered overview as you sew your quilt block really makes the whole process so much easier.

Remember: Paper piecing is done on the reverse side of the paper, so your finished block will be a mirror image of the numbered overview.

(continued)

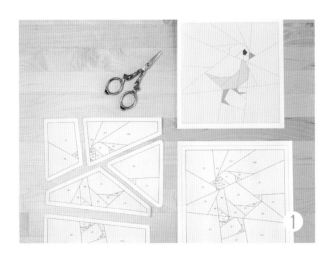

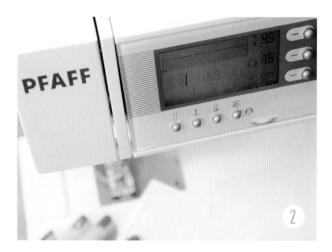

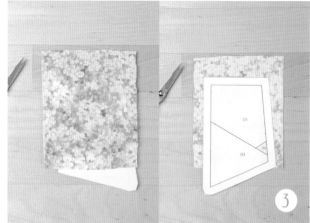

2. Set your machine stitch length to 16 to 18 stitches per inch or 1.5 stitches per centimeter. The stitches should be close together, so they perforate the paper nicely, but not too close, so they don't rip the paper. This will make it easy to remove the paper after you finish your block.

3. Turn the first segment over so the wrong side (unprinted side) is facing you. Place the piece of fabric for section 1 right side up, onto the paper, making sure there's ¼ to ½ inch (6 mm to 1.3 cm) of fabric around the perimeter of section 1.

Be generous in the beginning; once you are familiar with foundation paper piecing, you can cut your fabrics a bit smaller.

Pin or glue the fabric into place (I prefer to use a fabric glue pen so everything stays nicely in place; see page 12 for more details).

4. Turn the pattern segment over so the printed side is facing you. Fold the pattern on the line between sections 1 and 2. (I do this using a postcard; this gives you a nice straight and crisp fold.)

5. Trim fabric 1 to a ¼-inch (6-mm) seam allowance, using an acrylic ruler and rotary cutter (see page 12 for details on these tools).

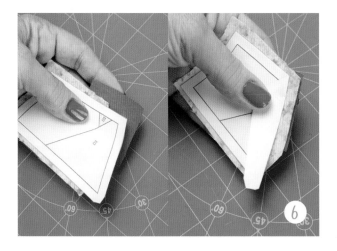

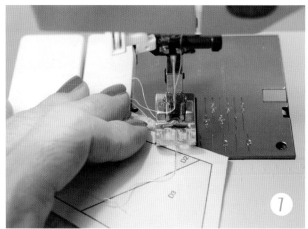

6. Choose the fabric for section 2 the same way you did for section 1, making sure the fabric covers the whole of section 2 and approximately ¼ to ½ inch (6 mm to 1.3 cm) around the perimeter of section 2.

   Place the right side of the fabric for section 2 together with the right side of fabric 1, aligning the raw edges of the two fabrics along the fold between sections 1 and 2.

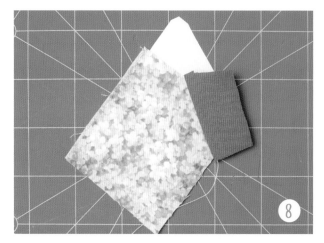

7. Now, stitch along the fold between sections 1 and 2, right on the line. The more precisely you sew, the easier it will be to align your segments! If the line that's being sewn starts or finishes at the ¼-inch (6-mm) seam allowance, extend that line right through the seam allowance by sewing all the way through it!

8. Flip open fabric 2 so the right sides of the fabrics are showing and press with a hot iron (no steam, as this can distort your fabric and paper; see page 11 for more information).

9. Now add the remaining pieces of fabric in numerical order, using the same method as in steps 4 to 8, folding the pattern at the line between sections 2 and 3 and so on.

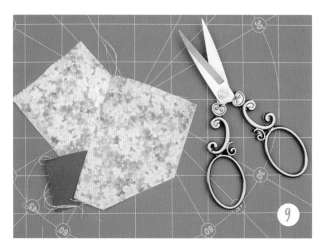

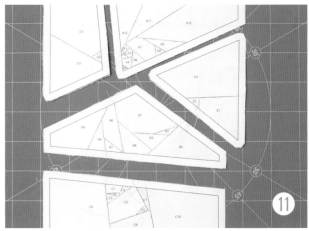

10. Sew each segment the same way. Then trim the fabric of each segment along the paper edge.

11. Place the trimmed segments as they are on the numbered overview. This just makes your life so much easier when sewing the segments together.

12. The segments should fit together perfectly; however, sometimes we're off a tiny bit with our stitching, so it's always important to double-check seams that need to match.

13. Pin these seams and double-check before stitching. This saves you from unpicking your seams.

ALIGN

ADORABLE ANIMAL QUILTING

14. Sew the segments together according to the assembly instructions in the pattern.

    After sewing two segments together, remove the paper only from the seam allowance and press the seams open with a hot iron (no steam) as flat as possible. This helps reduce bulk, especially when there are several layers of fabric. It also helps keep your overall size accurate.

15. After piecing all the segments, remove the remaining paper.

16. Use the iron to press your finished block.

FUSSY CUTTING

Fussy cutting means you're using a certain part of a print to showcase in your sewing. It is usually done using larger-scale and novelty prints, such as the seal in the water of my Olly the Orca block (page 141). It creates a really cute background for your blocks and makes an otherwise simple block more interesting.

I do this using my lightbox, but you can just as easily hold your fabric against any light. Place your fabric right side down and place your pattern template or segment on top, right side facing up. Pin or glue into place. Again, I prefer fabric glue so everything stays nicely in place. (See page 12 for more details.)

You can also use fussy cutting to give your animals a bit more life by using a dotted fabric for the eyes and placing the segment so the dot will become the pupil.

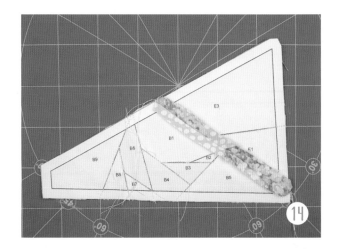

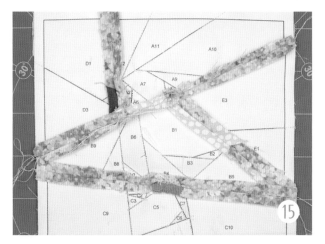

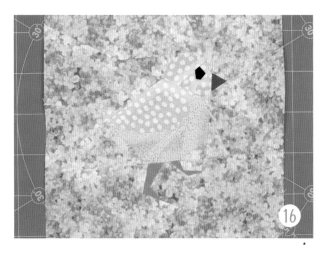

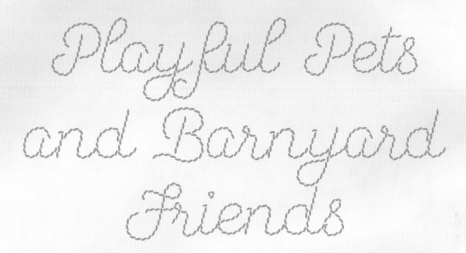

Playful Pets and Barnyard Friends

I was lucky enough to have had grandparents with a farm, so I was able to be on a farm frequently without having to do the hard work of maintaining and caring for it. So, in my head, a farm is still a wooden house in the midst of apple orchards, with tons of flowers in my grandma's garden and the smell of fresh apple pie.

All of my cute little pets and barnyard friends live on that farm in the south of Germany. No farm is complete without a cat and a dog, even though Dominic the Dog (page 21) is still a puppy. Donna the Donkey (page 29) might have helped in the old days with some chores, but nowadays is the main attraction for all the children. Pinkie the Pig (page 26) only lives on the farm for good luck. The chicken family (pages 30–33) provides fresh eggs, so Grandma can make the best apple pie in the whole wide world.

Inspired to make a cute farm animal quilt for your kids' bedroom or nursery? Or how about sewing a table runner with the chicken family on it? Pillowcases with Cammy the Cat (page 22) and Bell the Bunny (page 25) would be adorable, too.

Let's go farming . . . ah, I mean sewing. . . .

DOMINIC

DOMINIC THE DOG

QUILT BLOCK SIZE: 8 X 8 INCHES (20.3 X 20.3 CM)

A protective and courageous guard dog—that's what Dominic wants to be when he's grown up. But for now, he's just a little puppy who loves to hang out with his other barnyard friends. Running around and playing with the children is his favorite thing of all time.

This cute dog block would look fantastic on a backpack, pillowcase, fabric basket, lunch bag or even a whole quilt. This is a beginner-friendly pattern. But keep in mind that being precise and sewing right on the line makes it so much easier when joining the sections.

FABRIC NEEDED (YARDAGE BASED ON FABRIC WIDTH 44" TO 45" [112 TO 115 CM]):

- Light gray: ¼ yard (1 fat quarter) (46 x 56 cm)
- Mustard: ⅛ yard (1 fat eighth) (23 x 56 cm)
- Pink: about 5" x 5" (13 x 13 cm)
- Red: about 5" x 5" (13 x 13 cm)
- Black: about 5" x 5" (13 x 13 cm) (just the eye and nose)

ASSEMBLY INSTRUCTIONS

1. Begin by tracing or copying your templates (pages 36–37) onto your choice of paper, then cut out each section of the paper piecing pattern.

2. Sew each section as described in "Foundation Paper Piecing Made Easy" (page 13). Always refer to the numbered overview (page 35) when assembling the sections.

3. After joining the two sections, remove the paper only from the seam allowance and press your seams open as flat as possible with a hot, dry iron.

JOIN THE SECTIONS IN THE FOLLOWING ORDER

1. Sew together sections A and B and add section C to unit (A/B), followed by section D, then set aside.

2. Sew together sections G and H, then add section F to unit (G/H), followed by section E.

3. To finish, piece the head and body units together.

CAMMY THE CAT

QUILT BLOCK SIZE: 8 X 8 INCHES (20.3 X 20.3 CM)

This gracious feline is named Cammy. She loves to sit at the windowsill and watch people come and go. Cammy's dream life is cuddling up in a cozy little corner by the fireplace and sleeping all day.

A pretty sitting cat is the perfect decoration for a pillowcase, isn't it?

This pattern does have some small pieces. Be accurate when sewing and trimming your sections. Double-check the alignment before stitching two sections together; this saves you from unpicking your seams.

FABRIC NEEDED (YARDAGE BASED ON FABRIC WIDTH 44" TO 45" [112 TO 115 CM]):

- Pink: ¼ yard (1 fat quarter) (46 x 56 cm)
- Light gray: ⅛ yard (1 fat eighth) (23 x 56 cm)
- Dark gray: about 10" x 10" (26 x 26 cm)
- Pale gray: about 5" x 5" (13 x 13 cm)
- Rose: about 2" x 2" (5 x 5 cm) (just the nose)
- White: about 5" x 5" (13 x 13 cm)
- Black: about 5" x 5" (13 x 13 cm) (the black in the eyes)

Optional: Embroider some whiskers on the nose, using black embroidery thread and an embroidery needle.

ASSEMBLY INSTRUCTIONS

1. Start by tracing or copying your templates (pages 40–42) onto your choice of paper. Then, cut out each template of your pattern.

2. Sew each section as described in "Foundation Paper Piecing Made Easy" (page 13). Always refer to the numbered overview (page 39) when assembling the sections.

3. After joining two sections, remove the paper only from the seam allowance and press your seams open as flat as possible with a hot, dry iron.

JOIN THE SECTIONS IN THE FOLLOWING ORDER

1. Sew together sections A and B.

2. Sew together sections H and G and join (A/B) and (H/G).

3. Add section C to unit (A/B/H/G), followed by section E.

4. Then, add sections F and D to unit (A/B/H/G/C/E). Set aside.

5. Sew together sections J and I. Set aside.

6. Sew together sections K and L, then add section P to unit (K/L).

7. Next, add sections M, N, Q and O to unit (K/L/P), in that order.

8. Then, join unit (K/L/P/M/N/Q/O) with unit (J/I).

9. Now, stitch the head unit to the body unit.

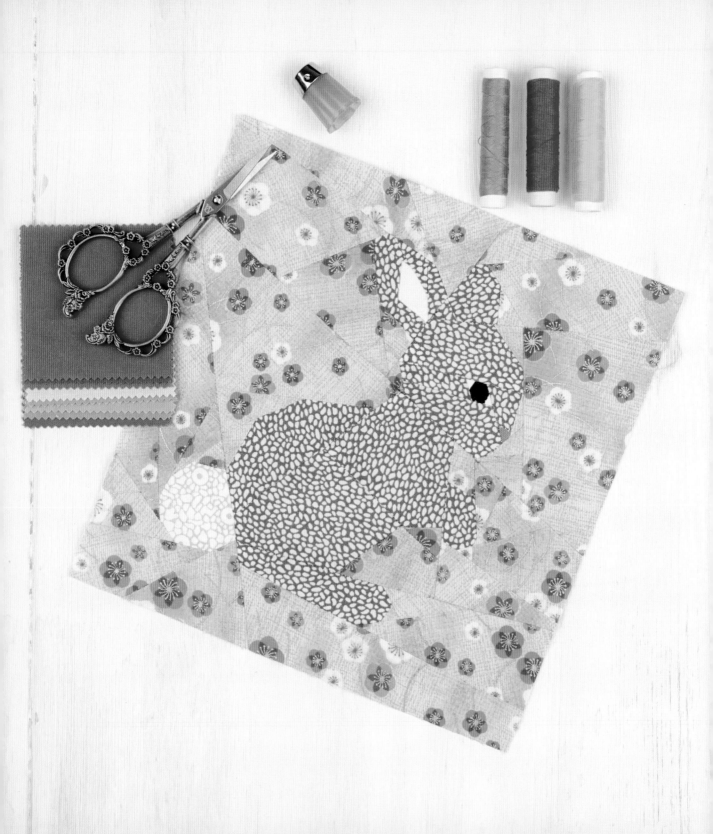

→ BELL THE BUNNY ←

QUILT BLOCK SIZE: 8 X 8 INCHES (20.3 X 20.3 CM)

Bell the Bunny is an exceptionally adorable barnyard friend that everyone loves to be around. Bell loves to play with the chickens on the farm. When small children approach her too fast, though, she becomes very skittish, as it's the one thing she really dislikes.

This pattern isn't just supercute for Easter; it can be used all year round for a lovely pillowcase, table runner or bunny quilt. A wall hanging made with this quilt block would be really adorable, too. Even if you frame this bunny block in a small hoop, it would make a sweet wall decoration.

FABRIC NEEDED (YARDAGE BASED ON FABRIC WIDTH 44" TO 45" [112 TO 115 CM]):

- Baby pink: ¼ yard (1 fat quarter) (46 x 56 cm)
- Light gray: ⅛ yard (1 fat eighth) (23 x 56 cm)
- White: about 5" x 5" (13 x 13 cm)
- Black: about 2" x 2" (5 x 5 cm) (just the eye)
- Sand: about 2" x 2" (5 x 5 cm) (just the nose)

ASSEMBLY INSTRUCTIONS

1. Trace or copy your pattern templates (pages 45–47) onto your choice of paper. Then, cut out these templates, using paper or craft scissors.

2. Sew each section as described in "Foundation Paper Piecing Made Easy" (page 13). Always refer to the numbered overview (page 44) when assembling the sections.

3. After joining the sections, remove the paper only from the seam allowance and press your seams open as flat as possible with a hot, dry iron.

JOIN THE SECTIONS IN THE FOLLOWING ORDER

1. Sew together sections A and B, then add sections D and E to unit (A/B).

2. Add section C at the top of unit (A/B/D/E) and section F to the side.

3. Next, join the ears of the bunny to the head by adding section G first to unit (A/B/D/E/C/F), followed by section H. Set aside.

4. Sew together sections J and I, then add sections L and K to unit (J/I).

5. Next, add section M and finally section N.

6. Now, join the head unit of the bunny to the body unit.

PINKIE THE PIG

QUILT BLOCK SIZE: 8 X 8 INCHES (20.3 X 20.3 CM)

Pinkie the Pig has lived on the farm for years. She loves spending her days rolling in the hay and mud and squeaking happily.

I like how versatile this pattern is. It can be made in all sorts of colors, depicting Pinkie just for fun and as a good-luck charm. No children's farm animal quilt would be complete without this fun block.

This is a great quilt block for beginners. When sewing your sections, make sure you sew right on the line. This ensures easy alignment of your sections when joining them.

FABRIC NEEDED (YARDAGE BASED ON FABRIC WIDTH 44" TO 45" [112 TO 115 CM]):

- Red: ¼ yard (1 fat quarter) (46 x 56 cm)

- Pink: ⅛ yard (1 fat eighth) (23 x 56 cm)

- Black: about 5" x 5" (13 x 13 cm)

ASSEMBLY INSTRUCTIONS

1. Begin by copying or tracing your pattern templates (pages 50–52) onto your choice of paper. Then, cut out your templates.

2. Sew each section as described in "Foundation Paper Piecing Made Easy" (page 13). Always refer to the numbered overview (page 49) when assembling the sections.

3. After joining the sections, remove the paper only from the seam allowance and press your seams open as flat as possible with a hot, dry iron.

JOIN THE SECTIONS IN THE FOLLOWING ORDER

1. Sew together sections A and D and add sections C and B to unit (A/D).

2. Now, add section E to unit (A/D/C/B), followed by sections L, M and N, in that order. Set aside.

3. Sew together sections G and F. Add section I to unit (G/F) and then section H.

4. Next, add section J to unit (G/F/I/H) and then section K.

5. To finish, piece the head and body halves together.

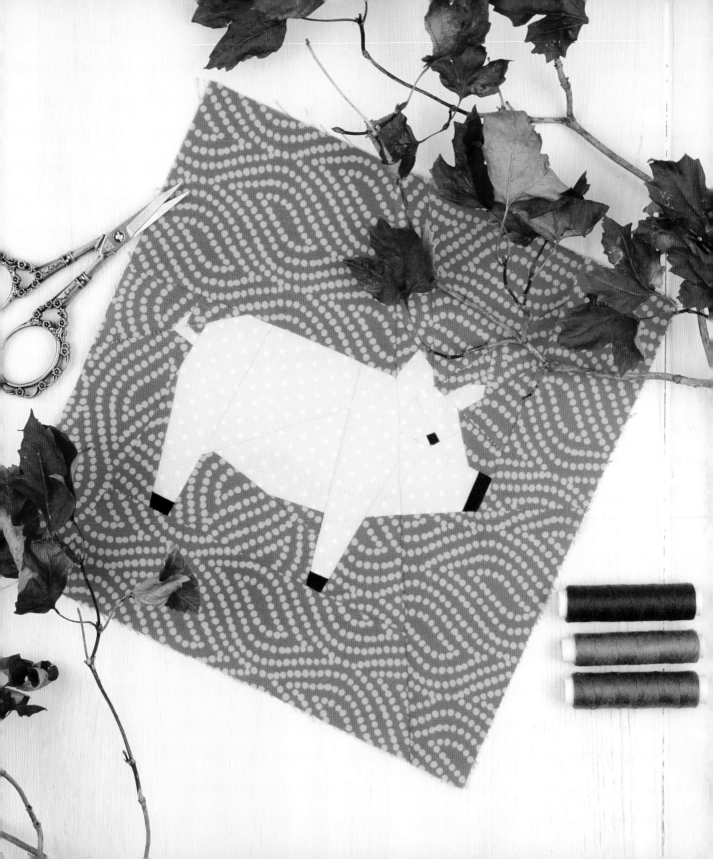

DONNA THE DONKEY

QUILT BLOCK SIZE: 8 X 8 INCHES (20.3 X 20.3 CM)

Because of her quiet and tolerant character, Donna the Donkey is extremely popular on the farm. She can carry heavy loads and probably made farmers' lives a lot easier in the olden days. Today, she endures all the kids wanting to ride on her back, without ever complaining.

This donkey block would complete any farm animal quilt for a children's room or nursery.

FABRIC NEEDED (YARDAGE BASED ON FABRIC WIDTH 44" TO 45" [112 TO 115 CM]):

- Yellow: ¼ yard (1 fat quarter) (46 x 56 cm)
- Gray: ⅛ yard (1 fat eighth) (23 x 56 cm)
- Light gray: about 5" x 5" (13 x 13 cm) (just the ear)
- Black: about 5" x 5" (13 x 13 cm)
- Dark gray: about 5" x 5" (13 x 13 cm)
- Sand: about 5" x 5" (13 x 13 cm)

ASSEMBLY INSTRUCTIONS

1. Before you start sewing each section of this block, trace or copy your pattern templates (pages 55–57) onto your choice of paper. Then, cut out these templates and sew them according to "Foundation Paper Piecing Made Easy" (page 13). Always refer to the numbered overview (page 54) when assembling the sections.

2. After joining the sections, remove the paper only from the seam allowance and press your seams open as flat as possible with a hot, dry iron.

JOIN THE SECTIONS IN THE FOLLOWING ORDER

1. Sew together sections A and B.

2. Add section E to unit (A/B), followed by sections D and C. Set aside.

3. Sew together sections G and H, add section I to unit (G/H), then add section F, followed by section J. Set aside.

4. Sew together sections K and L, then add section M. Now, add section N to unit (K/L/M), followed by section O at the bottom and section P at the top.

5. To finish, piece the head unit of the donkey (A/B/E/D/C) and chest unit (G/H/I/F/J) together and join this unit with the body of the donkey (K/L/M/N/O/P).

BABY CHICK

QUILT BLOCK SIZE: 6 X 6 INCHES (15.2 X 15.2 CM)

Baby Chick lives with her mama and daddy, the handsome rooster, on a small farm outside the big city, far away from the noise and smell of too many cars and not enough trees.

Baby Chick would look fantastic in a quilt with all the other farm animals, or she would be stunning on a table runner with the rest of her chicken family.

This pattern is very beginner-friendly.

Precision makes your life a lot easier. Make sure you sew straight on the line. Refer to the numbered overview (page 59) when assembling your segments. And double-check the alignment before stitching; this saves you from unpicking your seams.

FABRIC NEEDED (YARDAGE BASED ON FABRIC WIDTH 44" TO 45" [112 TO 115 CM]):

- Pink: ⅛ yard (1 fat eighth) (23 x 56 cm)
- Light yellow: about 10" x 10" (26 x 26 cm)
- Dark yellow: about 5" x 5" (13 x 13 cm)
- Red: about 2" x 2" (5 x 5 cm) (just the beak)
- Orange: about 5" x 5" (13 x 13 cm)
- Black: about 2" x 2" (5 x 5 cm) (just the eye)

ASSEMBLY INSTRUCTIONS

1. Begin this cute block by copying or tracing the pattern templates (page 60) onto your choice of paper. Then, cut out the templates.

2. Now, sew each section of the pattern according to "Foundation Paper Piecing Made Easy" (page 13). Always refer to the numbered overview (page 59) when assembling the sections.

3. After joining the sections, remove the paper only from the seam allowance and press your seams open as flat as possible with a hot, dry iron.

JOIN THE SECTIONS IN THE FOLLOWING ORDER

1. Sew together sections A and D.

2. Sew together sections B and E, then add section C to unit (B/E).

3. To finish, piece the top and bottom halves together.

MAMA CHICKEN

QUILT BLOCK SIZE: 8 X 8 INCHES (20.3 X 20.3 CM)

This pretty Mama Chicken is keeping an eye on her baby, just as any mama does. She's looking after her little one with love and devotion. And she provides eggs for Granny's apple pie.

Mama Chicken would look fantastic with her other barnyard friends in a farm animal quilt. It would also work beautifully as a table runner for Easter featuring the whole chicken family.

This pattern is for the intermediate quilter. It has some small pieces, so precision is important. It helps to double-check the alignment before joining two sections. It's always better than unpicking your seams.

FABRIC NEEDED (YARDAGE BASED ON FABRIC WIDTH 44" TO 45" [112 TO 115 CM]):

- Green: ¼ yard (1 fat quarter) (46 x 56 cm)
- Cream: ⅛ yard (1 fat eighth) (23 x 56 cm)
- Light yellow: about 10" x 10" (26 x 26 cm)
- Red: about 5" x 5" (13 x 13 cm)
- Orange: about 5" x 5" (13 x 13 cm)
- Black: about 2" x 2" (5 x 5 cm)

ASSEMBLY INSTRUCTIONS

1. Start this quilt block by copying or tracing your pattern templates (pages 63–65) onto your choice of paper. Then, cut out those templates.

2. Sew each section as described in "Foundation Paper Piecing Made Easy" (page 13). Always refer to the numbered overview (page 62) when assembling the sections.

3. After joining two sections, remove the paper only from the seam allowance and press your seams open as flat as possible with a hot, dry iron.

JOIN THE SECTIONS IN THE FOLLOWING ORDER

1. Sew together sections B and C, add section D to unit (B/C), then join section A to unit (B/C/D) followed by section E. Set aside.

2. Sew together sections H and G, then add section F to unit (H/G), followed by section I.

3. Sew together sections K and L, then add section M to unit (K/L), followed by section J.

4. Join unit (H/G/F/I) with unit (K/L/M/J).

5. To finish, piece the head and body halves together.

⇁ ROOSTER ↽

QUILT BLOCK SIZE: 8 X 8 INCHES (20.3 X 20.3 CM)

Look at this handsome Rooster. It's easy to say he's the best-looking rooster on the farm . . . well, yes—he's also the only one. He loves parading around the farm and impressing his hen and chicks.

This pattern looks more complicated than it actually is. It has some small pieces, though, so precision is very important.

This rooster would look fabulous on a bag. A wall hanging with the rest of the chicken family would be equally adorable. Or how about placemats with each of the chicken family members?

This is a scrap-friendly pattern, so check out your leftover fabrics.

FABRIC NEEDED (YARDAGE BASED ON FABRIC WIDTH 44" TO 45" [112 TO 115 CM]):

- Gray: ¼ yard (1 fat quarter) (46 x 56 cm)
- 4 different green fabrics: each about 5" x 5" (13 x 13 cm)
- 4 different blue fabrics: each about 5" x 5" (13 x 13 cm)
- 6 different red fabrics: each about 5" x 5" (13 x 13 cm)
- Yellow: about 5" x 5" (13 x 13 cm)
- Orange: about 5" x 5" (13 x 13 cm)
- Black: about 2" x 2" (5 x 5 cm) (just the eye)

ASSEMBLY INSTRUCTIONS

1. Before you start sewing this awesome rooster, copy or trace the pattern templates (pages 68–69) onto your choice of paper and cut out the pattern templates.

2. Sew each section as described in "Foundation Paper Piecing Made Easy" (page 13). Precision is key with foundation paper piecing, and sewing straight on the pattern line makes your assembly a whole lot easier.

   Always refer to the numbered overview (page 67) when assembling the sections.

3. After joining two sections, remove the paper only from the seam allowance and press your seams open as flat as possible with a hot, dry iron.

JOIN THE SECTIONS IN THE FOLLOWING ORDER

1. Sew together sections A and B, then add section D to unit (A/B), followed by section C.

2. Sew together sections F and G, then add section H to unit (F/G), followed by section E.

3. Sew together sections J and I, then add section K.

4. Now, join unit (J/I/K) with unit (F/G/H/E) and add unit (A/B/D/C).

5. To finish, piece the tail, section L, to the body of the rooster.

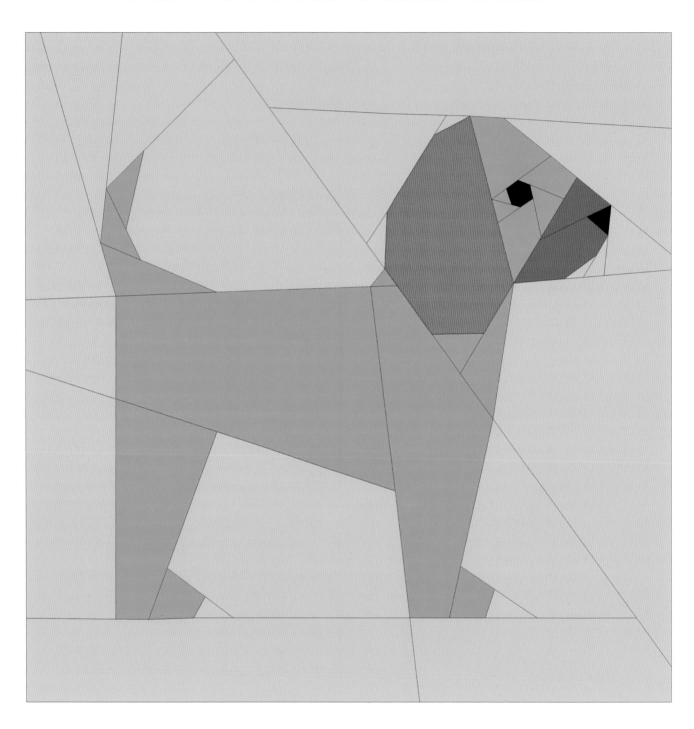

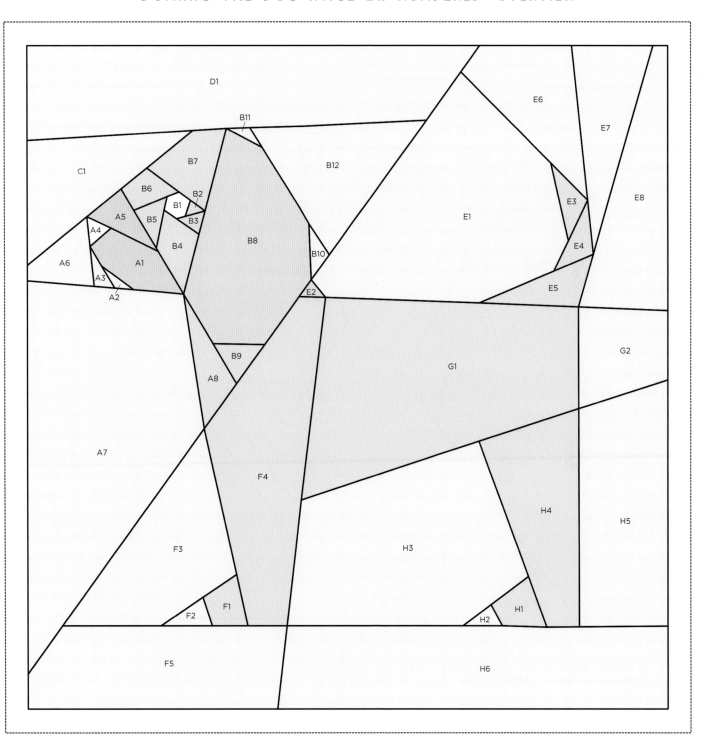

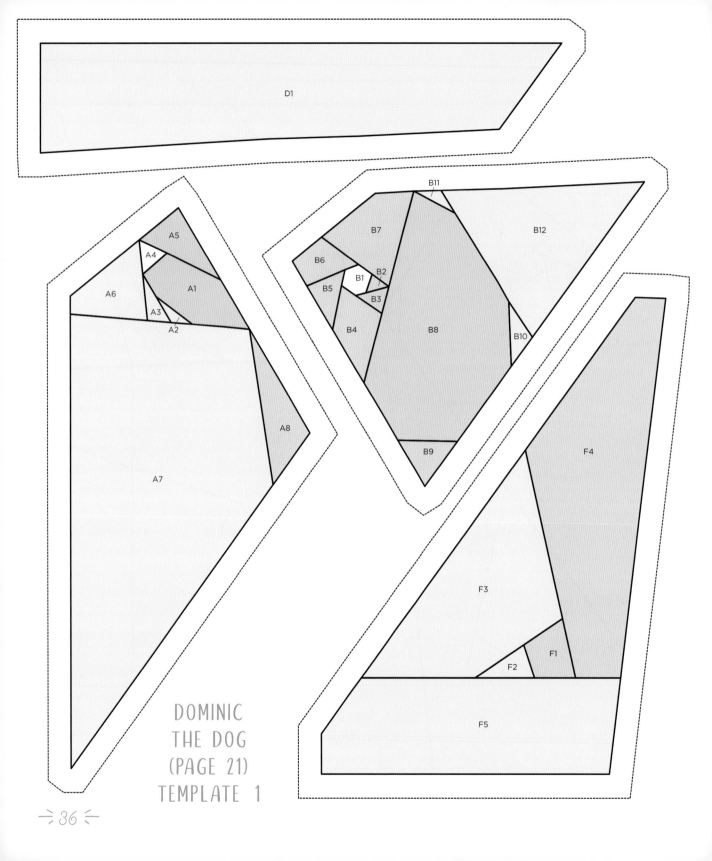

DOMINIC
THE DOG
(PAGE 21)
TEMPLATE 1

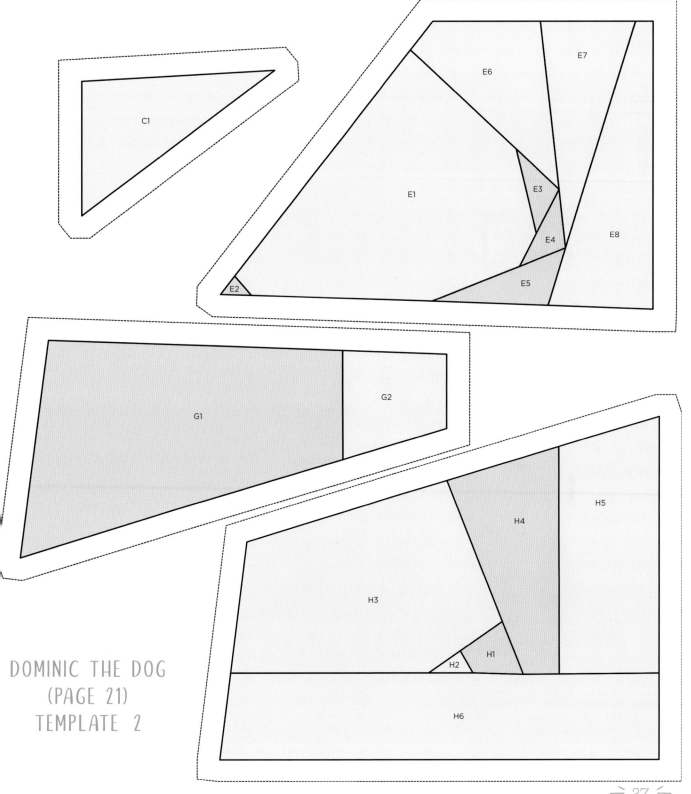

DOMINIC THE DOG
(PAGE 21)
TEMPLATE 2

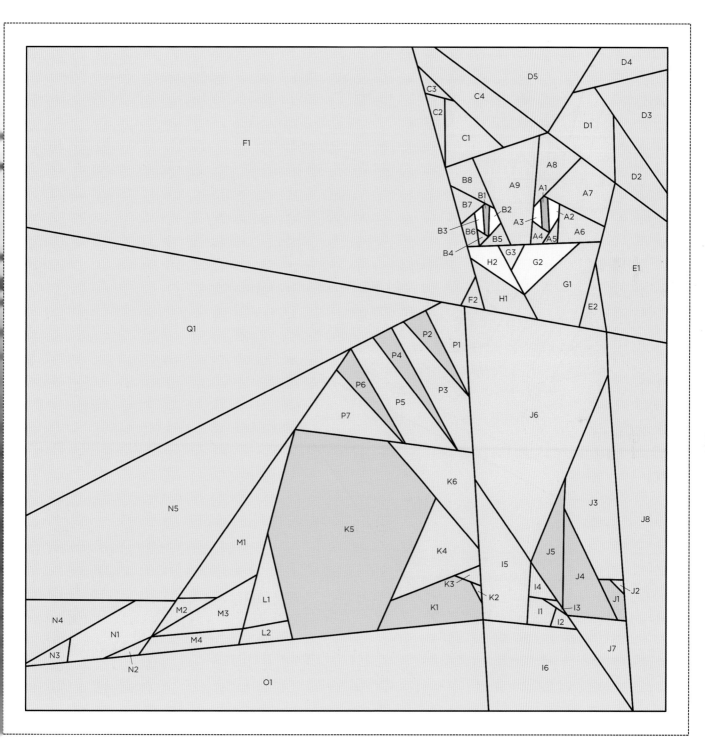

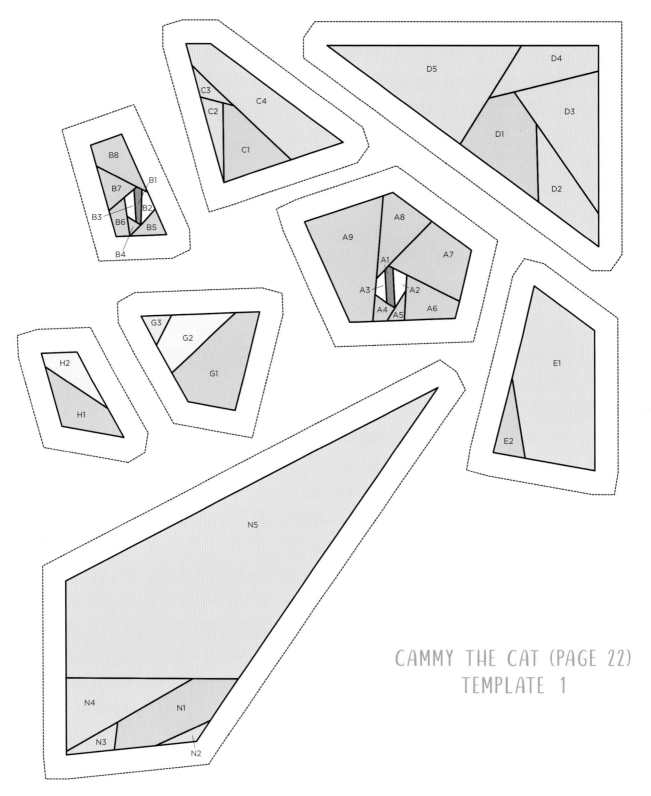

CAMMY THE CAT (PAGE 22)
TEMPLATE 1

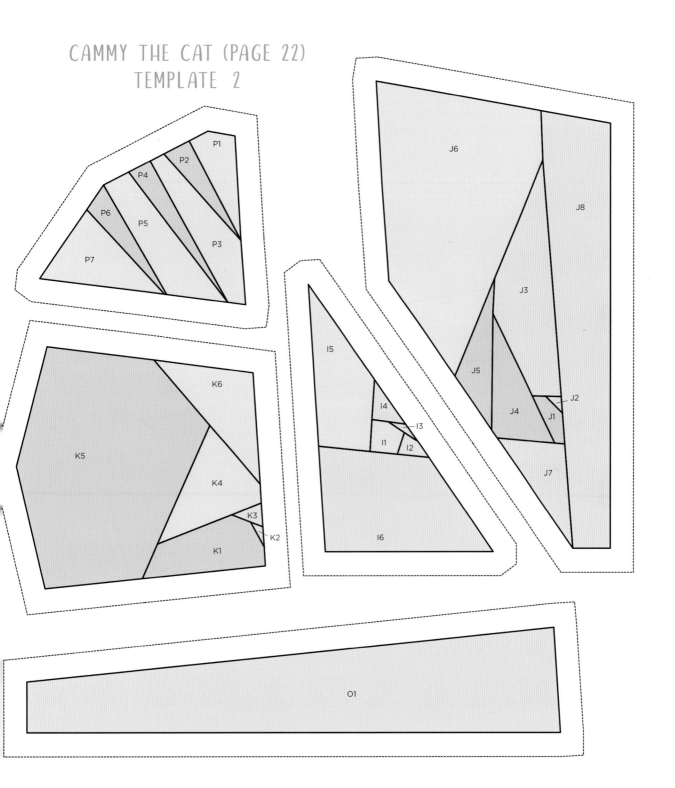

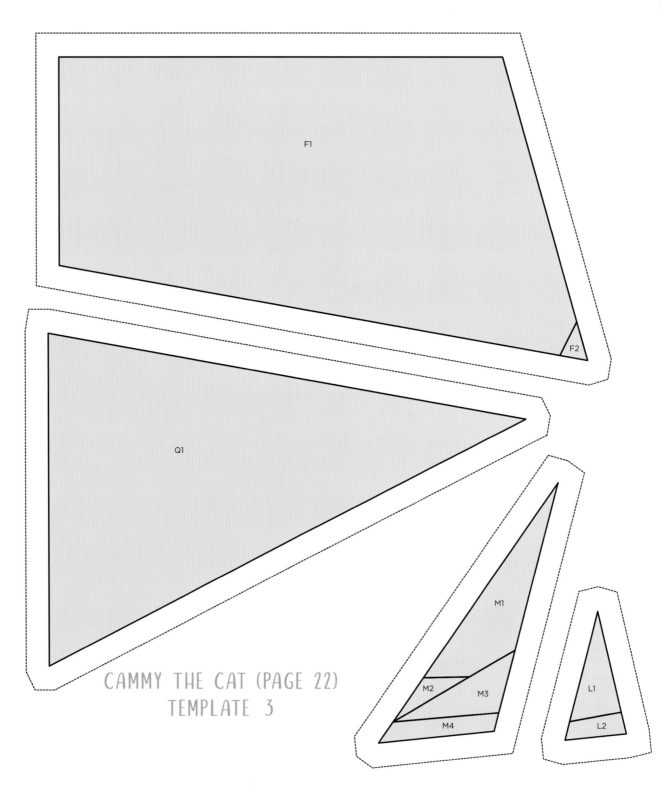

CAMMY THE CAT (PAGE 22)
TEMPLATE 3

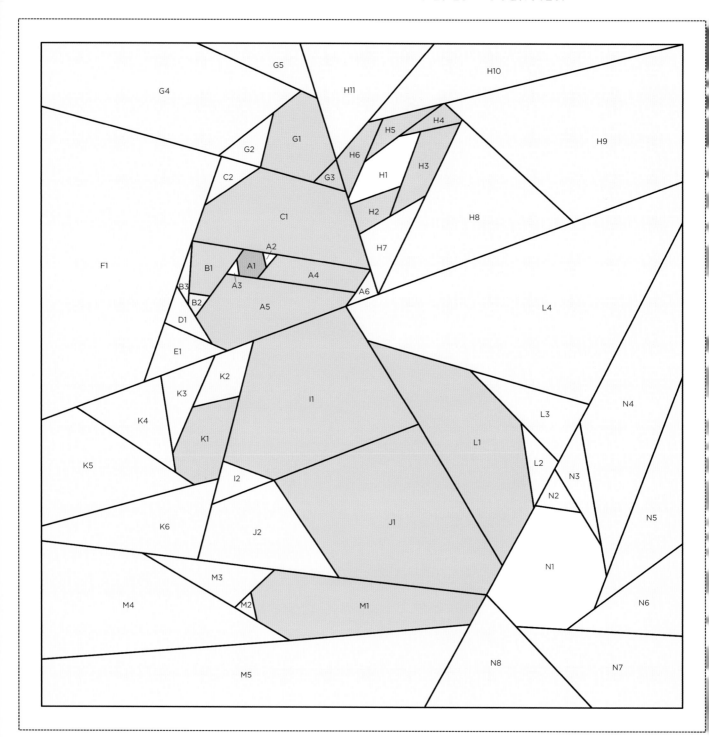

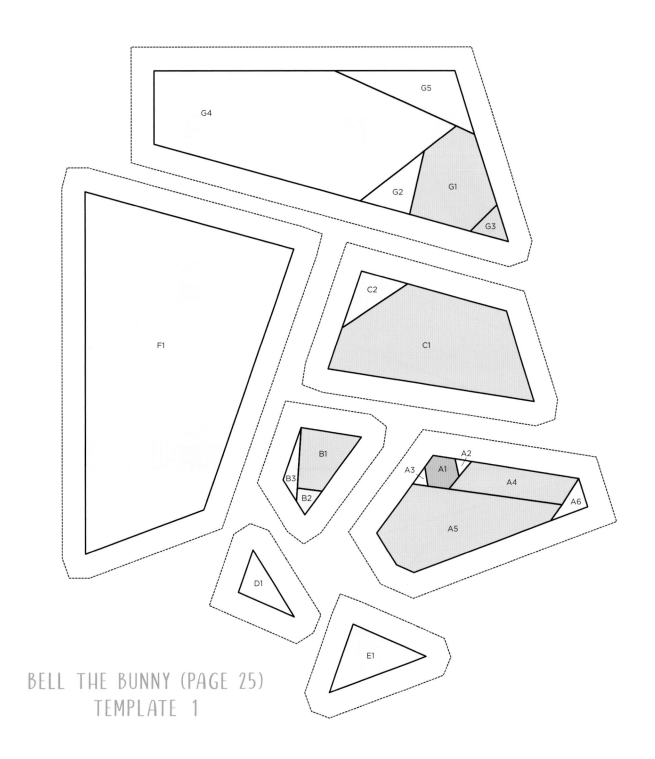

BELL THE BUNNY (PAGE 25)
TEMPLATE 1

BELL THE BUNNY
(PAGE 25)
TEMPLATE 2

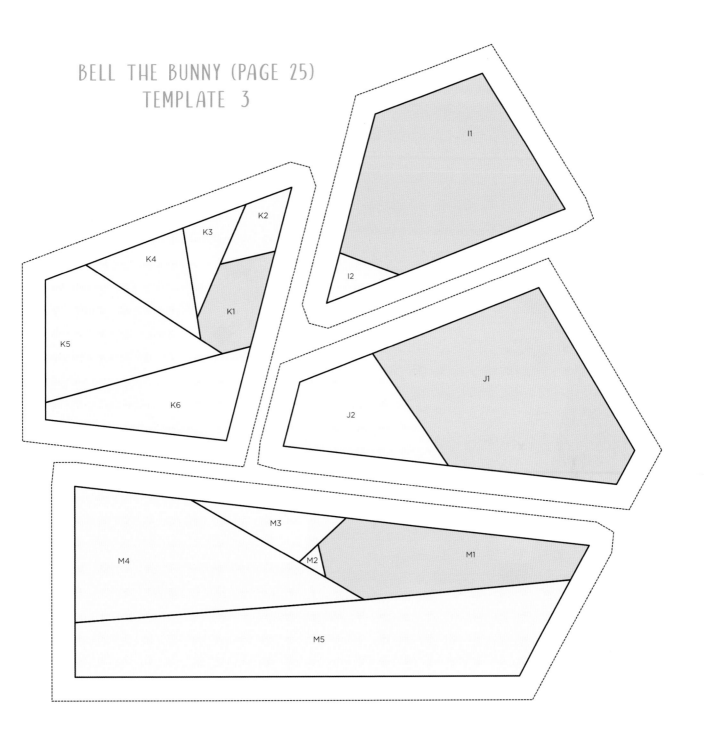

BELL THE BUNNY (PAGE 25)
TEMPLATE 3

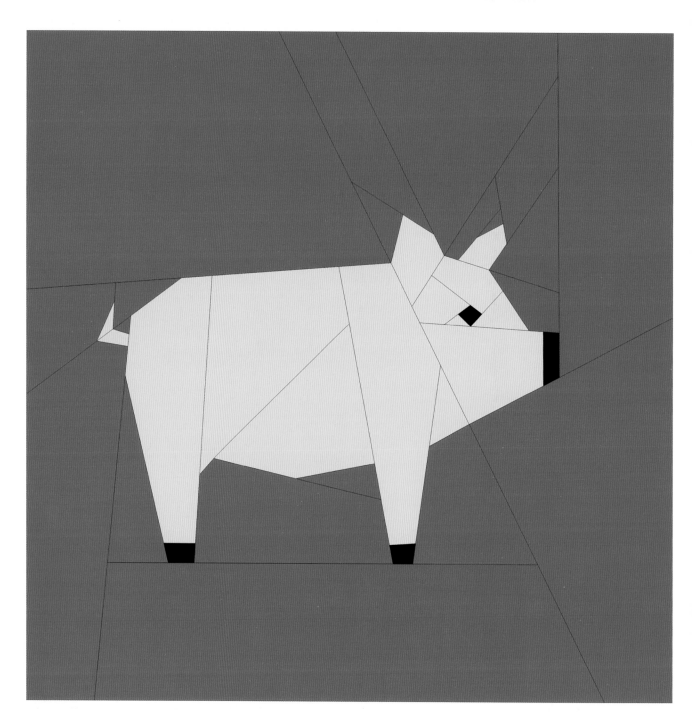

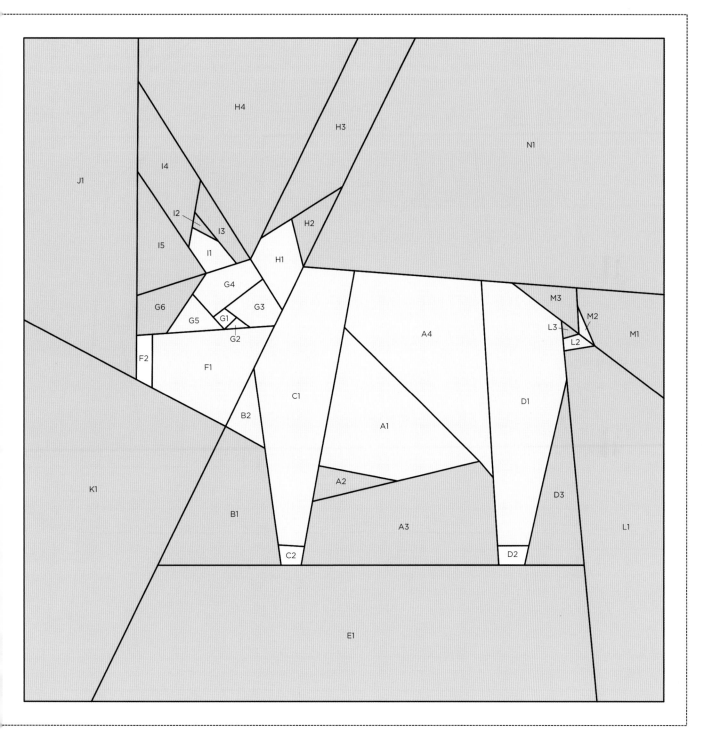

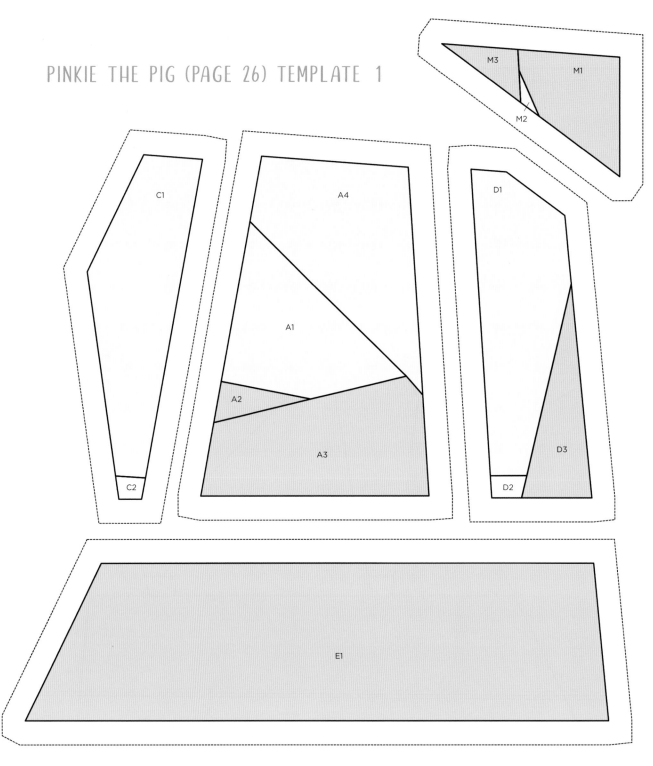

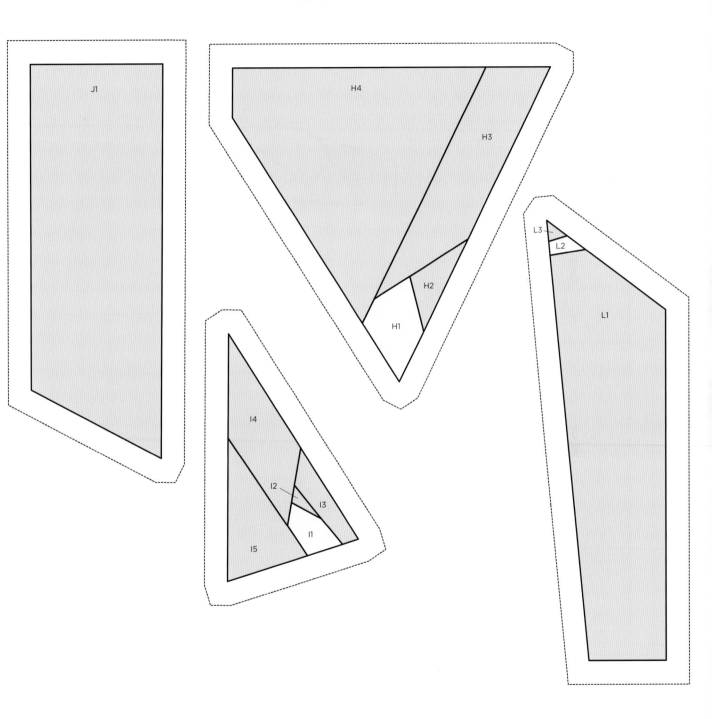

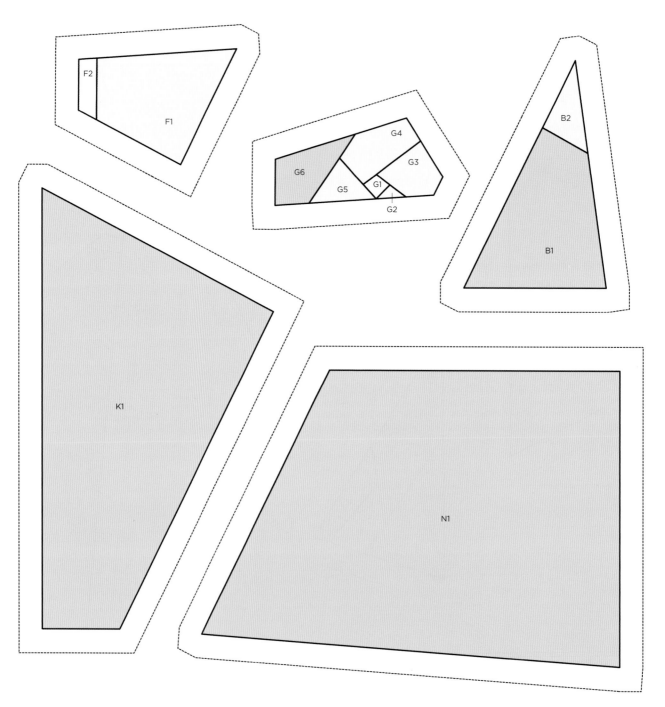

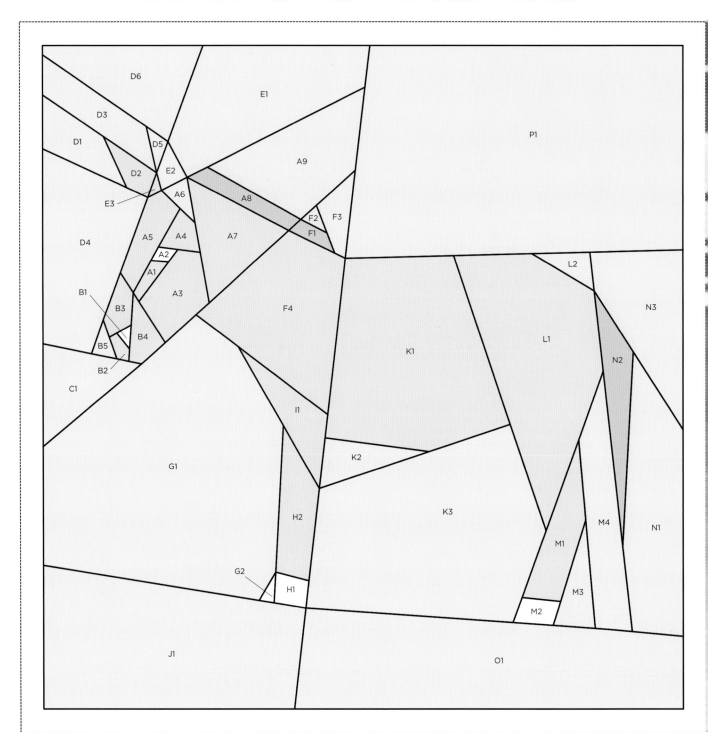

DONNA THE DONKEY
(PAGE 29)
TEMPLATE 1

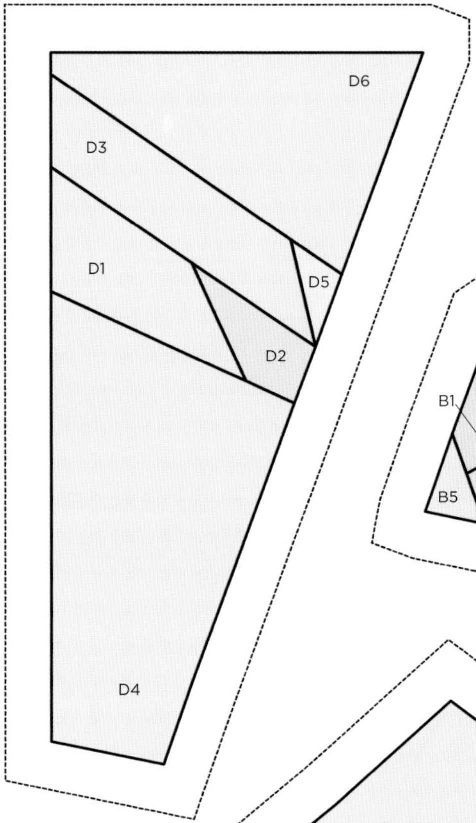

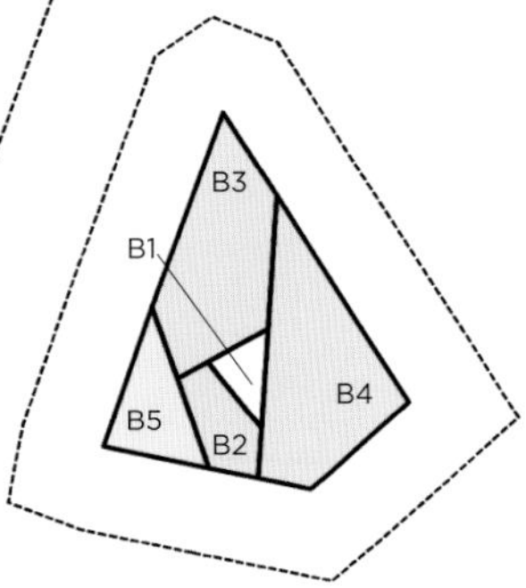

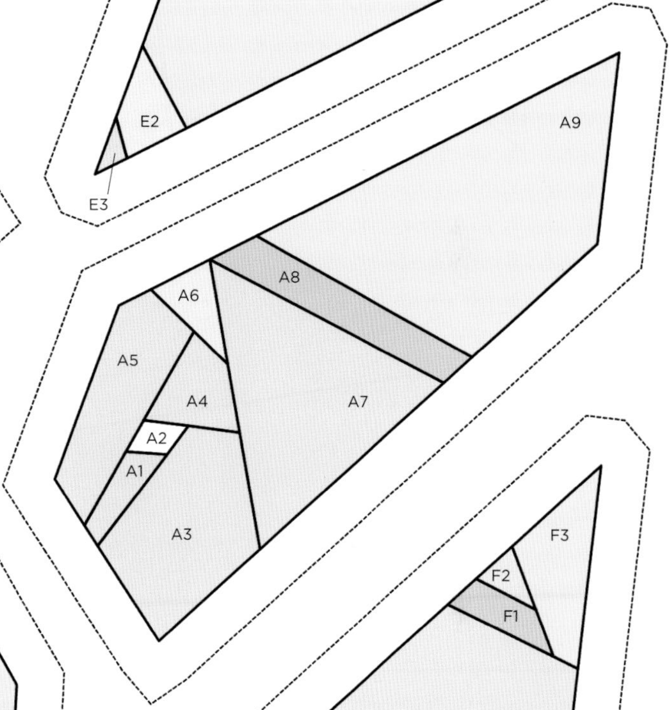

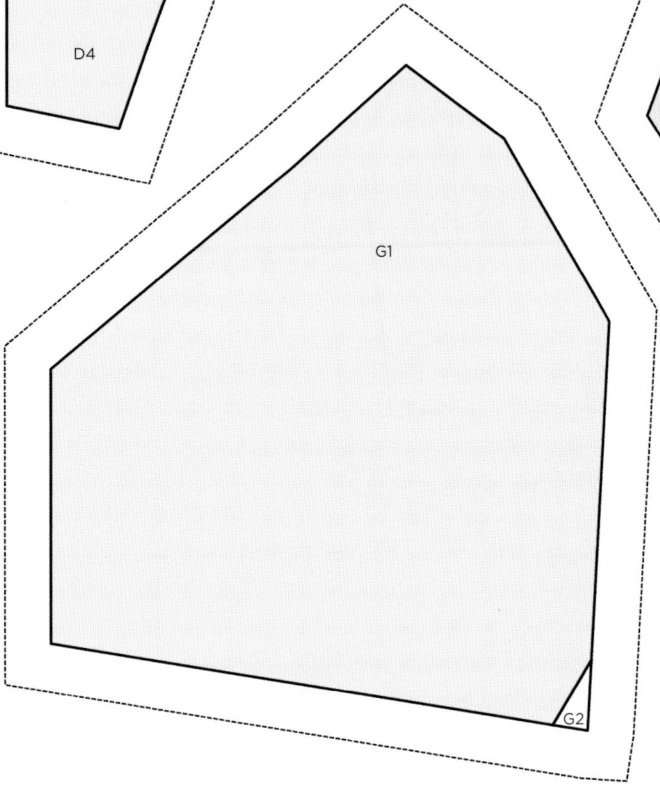

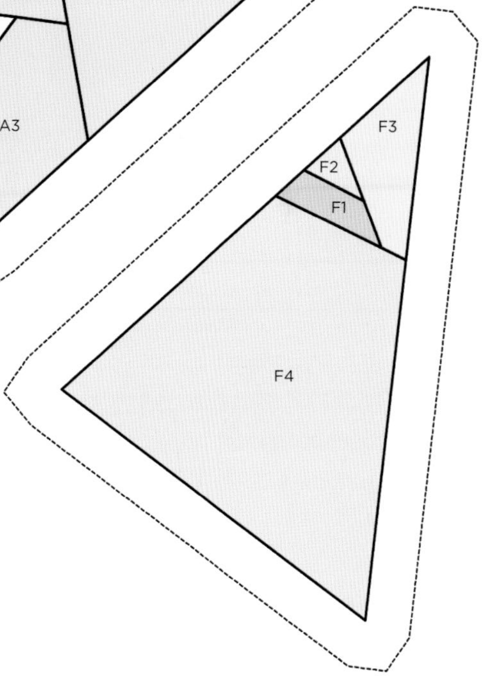

D6

D3

D1

D5

D2

D4

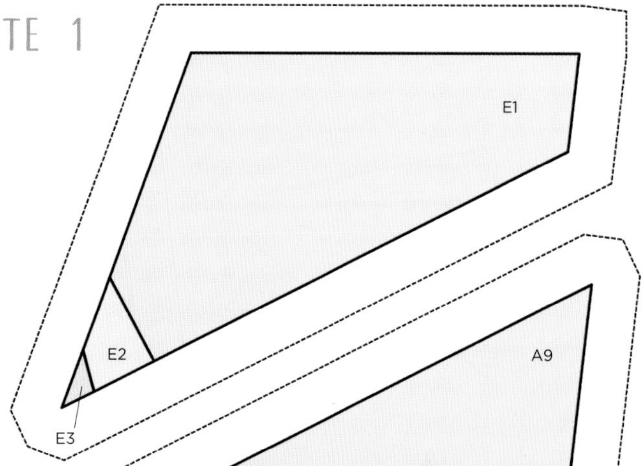

B3

B1

B5 B2 B4

E1

E2

E3

A9

A6 A8

A5

A4 A7

A2

A1

A3

F3

F2

F1

F4

G1

G2

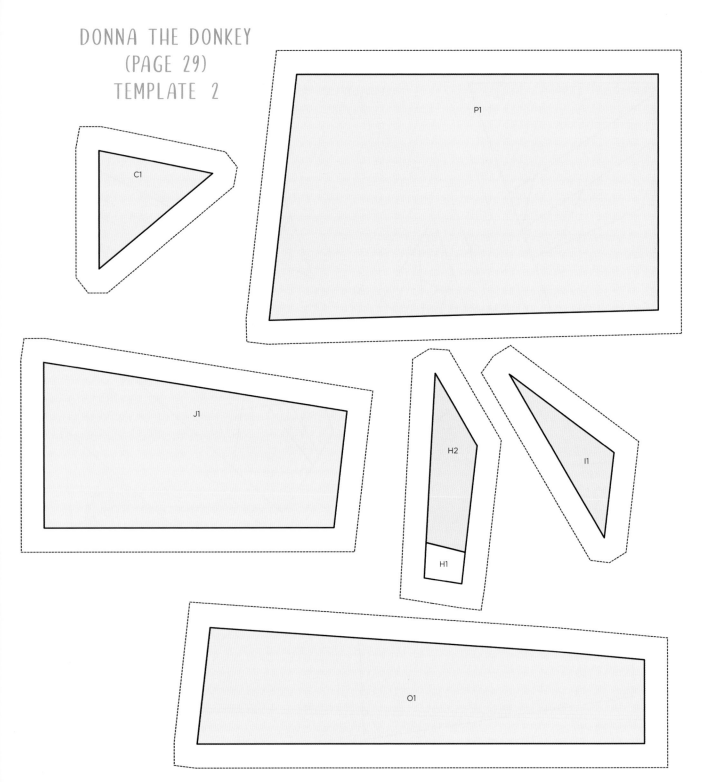

DONNA THE DONKEY
(PAGE 29)
TEMPLATE 2

C1

P1

J1

H2

I1

H1

O1

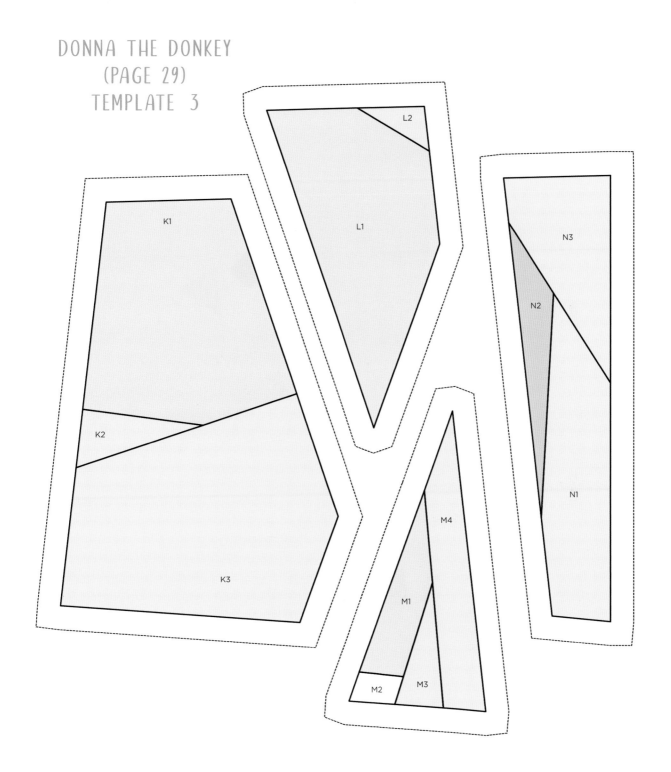

DONNA THE DONKEY
(PAGE 29)
TEMPLATE 3

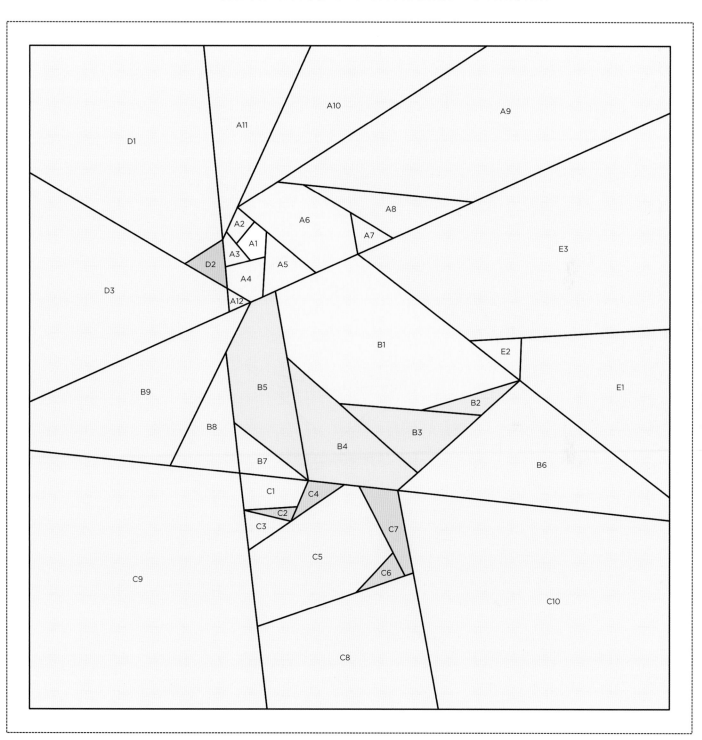

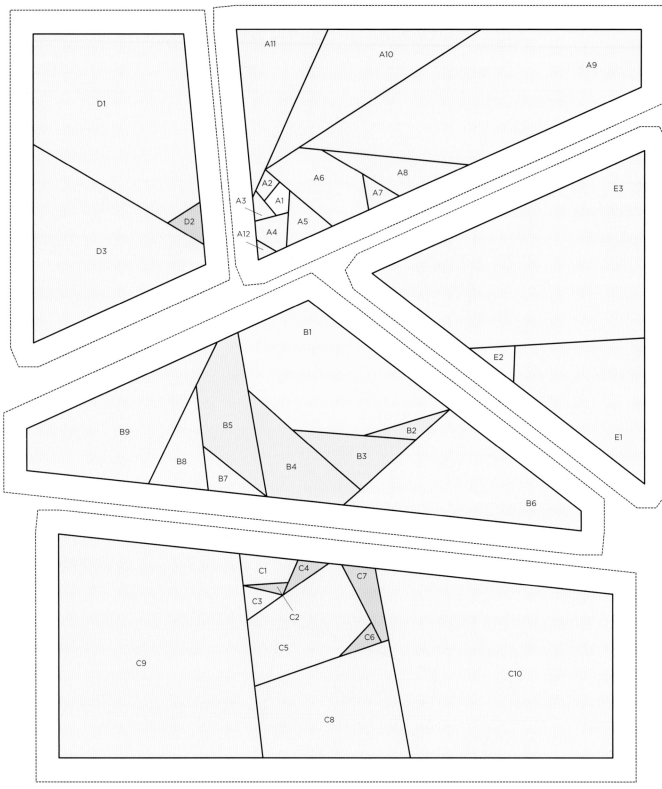

BABY CHICK (PAGE 30) TEMPLATE

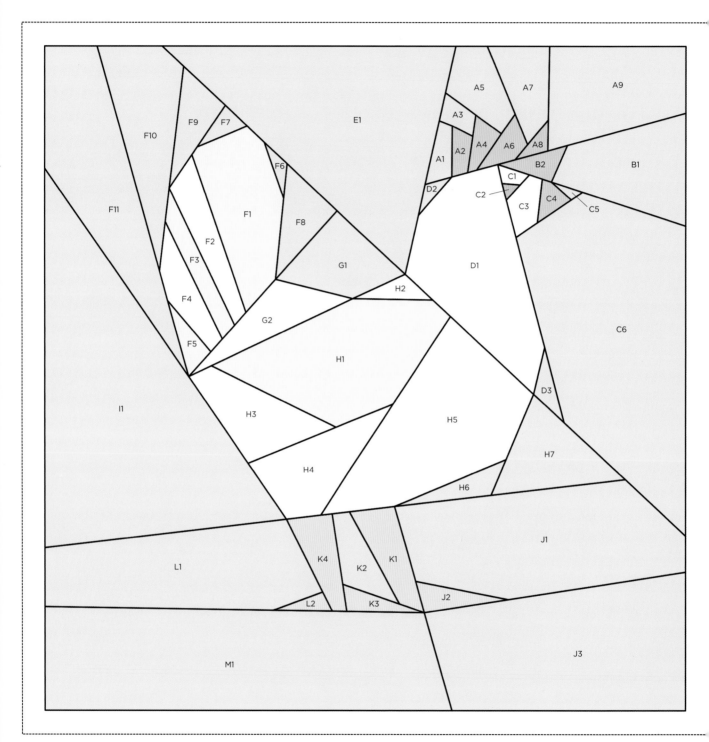

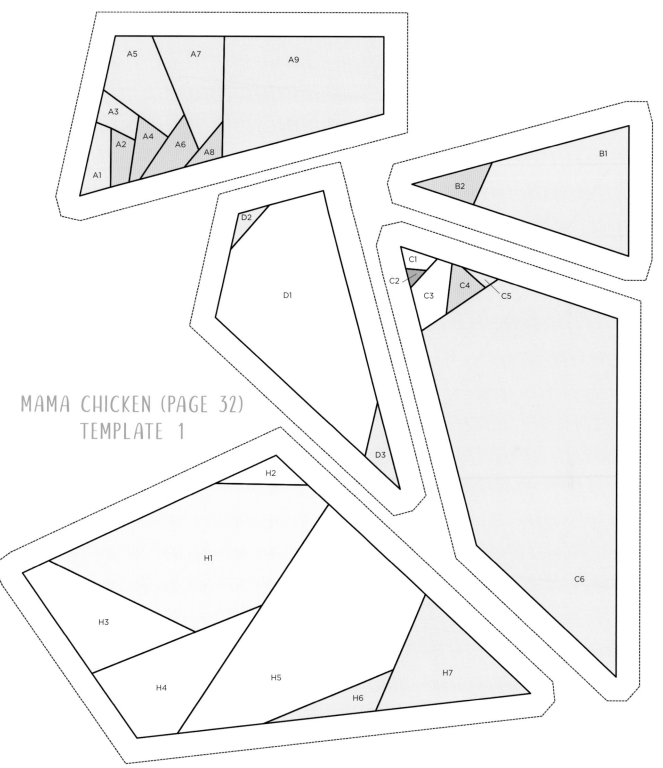

MAMA CHICKEN (PAGE 32)
TEMPLATE 1

A5 A7 A9
A3 A4 A6 A8
A2 A1

B1 B2

D2 D1 D3

C1 C2 C3 C4 C5 C6

H2 H1 H3 H4 H5 H6 H7

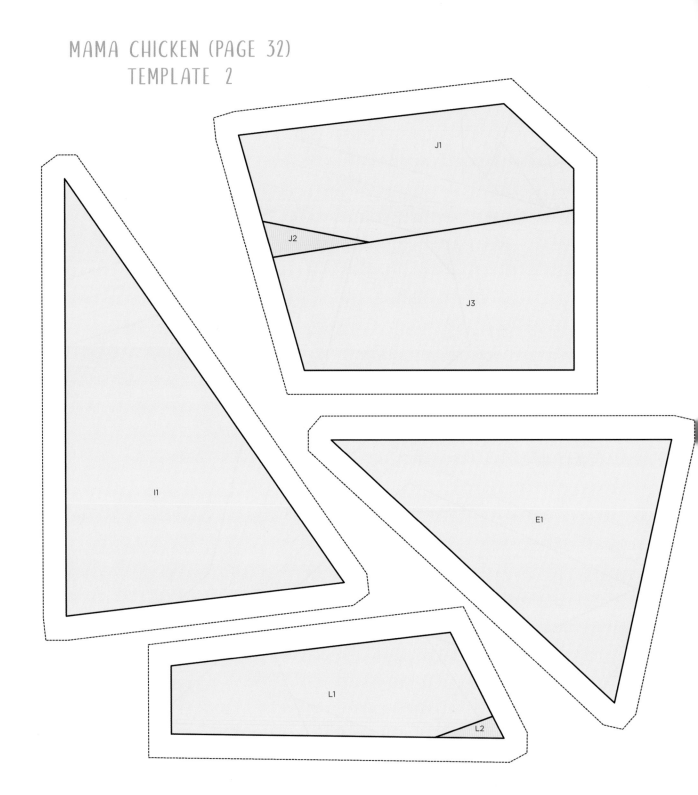

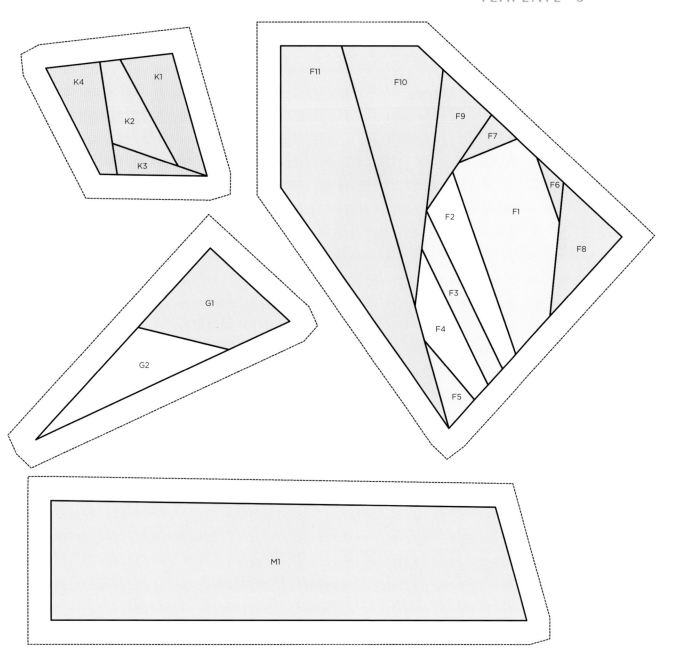

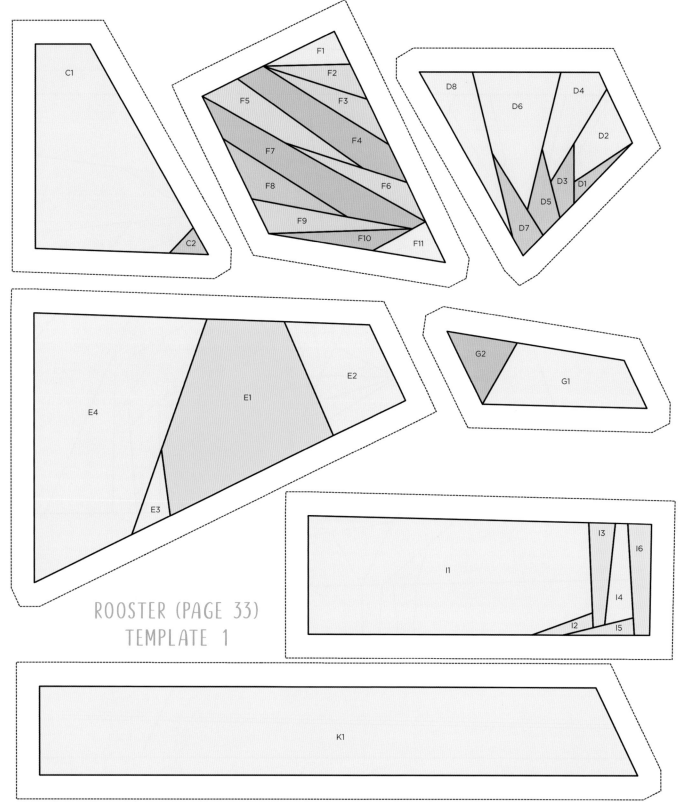

ROOSTER (PAGE 33)
TEMPLATE 1

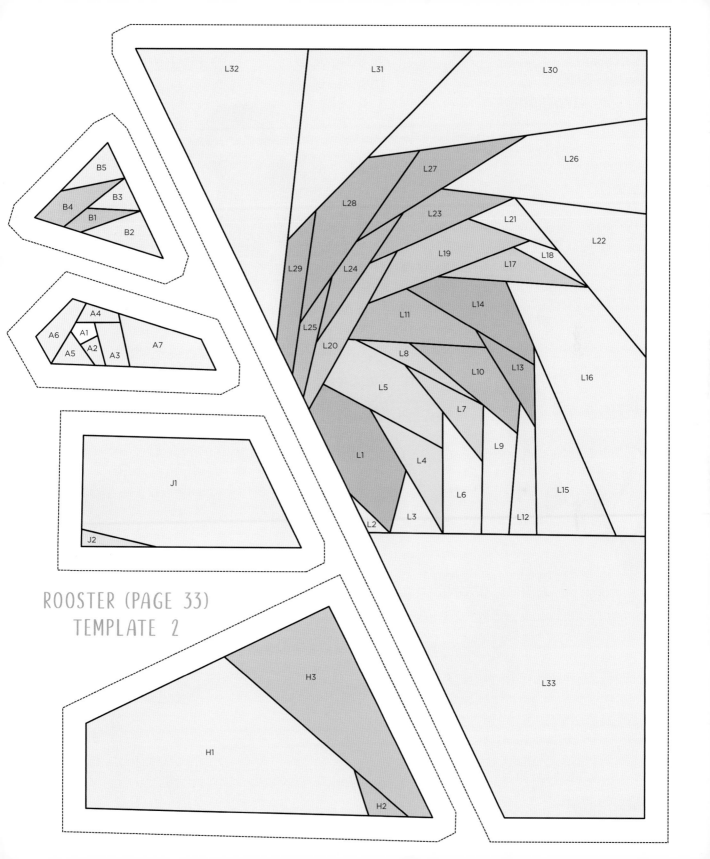

ROOSTER (PAGE 33)
TEMPLATE 2

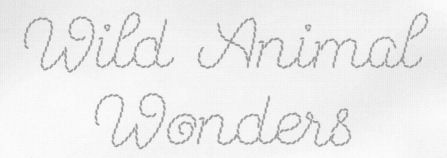

Wild Animal Wonders

These quilt blocks were inspired by many of my travels across the globe. Whether it was the Andes Mountains in Colombia for Ali the Alpaca (page 73), or the Nile River in Egypt for Craig the Crocodile (page 74), each animal reminds me of one of many journeys. I designed these quilt blocks so you can bring a little bit of the wild animal kingdom to your home. With so many beautiful and amazing animals in this world, it was really hard to choose. I'm sure you will like my selection.

There are numerous ways for these blocks to be used. Maybe you want a memory of your last exotic holiday and Michael the Monkey (page 77) reminds you of your vacation. Or you want to make an animal quilt for your child's bedroom. Toni the Toucan (page 82) would be really stunning on a pillowcase.

Whatever it is you decide to make with these blocks, they will certainly take you to the amazing places where these animals live in their natural habitat.

So, let the journey begin. Choose your first wild animal, select the matching fabric and let's go travel . . . to your sewing machine.

⇥ ALI THE ALPACA ⇤

QUILT BLOCK SIZE: 8 X 8 INCHES (20.3 X 20.3 CM)

Ali the Alpaca is often called a llama and she doesn't like that at all, since she's way smaller than a llama and has softer, fluffier and curlier hair. Also, her face is so much cuter. She produces one of the finest wools you can find; it's incredibly soft and wonderful to wear, so how can anyone possibly mistake her for a llama?

This pattern is for the advanced quilter since it has many small pieces that require considerable precision. Be careful and accurate when sewing and trimming your sections. Double-check the alignment before stitching two sections together; this saves you from unpicking your seams.

FABRIC NEEDED (YARDAGE BASED ON FABRIC WIDTH 44" TO 45" [112 TO 115 CM]):

- Baby blue: ¼ yard (1 fat quarter) (46 x 56 cm)
- Cream: about 10" x 10" (26 x 26 cm)
- Orange: about 5" x 5" (13 x 13 cm)
- Pink: about 5" x 5" (13 x 13 cm)
- Yellow: about 5" x 5" (13 x 13 cm)
- Red: about 5" x 5" (13 x 13 cm)
- Black: about 5" x 5" (13 x 13 cm)
- Taupe: about 2" x 2" (5 x 5 cm) (just the face)

ASSEMBLY INSTRUCTIONS

1. Start by tracing or copying your pattern templates (pages 90–92) onto your choice of paper.

2. Then, cut out your pattern templates and sew each section as described in "Foundation Paper Piecing Made Easy" (page 13). Refer to the numbered overview (page 89) when assembling the sections.

3. After joining two sections, remove the paper only from the seam allowance and press your seams open as flat as possible with a hot, dry iron.

JOIN THE SECTIONS IN THE FOLLOWING ORDER

1. Sew together sections A, B and C, then add section D to unit (A/B/C), followed by section E.

2. Now, add section H to unit (A/B/C/D/E), followed by sections I and J. Set aside.

3. Sew together sections M and L.

4. Sew together sections O and P, then add sections N, K and Q, in that order, to unit (O/P).

5. Sew together sections G and F.

6. Now join units (M/L), (O/P/N/K/Q) and (G/F).

7. Piece the front/head unit and body unit together.

CRAIG THE CROCODILE

QUILT BLOCK SIZE: 8 X 8 INCHES (20.3 X 20.3 CM)

Craig the Crocodile lives in extremely warm areas and loves salt water as much as freshwater. He spends all day rolling in the mud, taking swims and lazing in the sun . . . a perfect life! This pattern captures Craig in his full appearance.

I like how versatile this pattern is. It can be made with blues, greens or even browns as a background, depicting the animal either in water or on land.

This crocodile block would look fantastic on a backpack, pillowcase, fabric basket, lunch bag or even a whole quilt.

FABRIC NEEDED (YARDAGE BASED ON FABRIC WIDTH 44" TO 45" [112 TO 115 CM]):

- Light turquoise: ¼ yard (1 fat quarter) (46 x 56 cm)
- Green: ⅛ yard (1 fat eighth) (23 x 56 cm)
- Teal: about 10" x 10" (26 x 26 cm)
- Salmon: about 10" x 10" (26 x 26 cm)
- White: about 10" x 10" (26 x 26 cm)
- Black: about 2" x 2" (5 x 5 cm) (just the eye)

ASSEMBLY INSTRUCTIONS

1. Copy or trace the templates (pages 95–97) onto your choice of paper. Cut out the templates and sew each section as described in "Foundation Paper Piecing Made Easy" (page 13). Refer to the numbered overview (page 94) when assembling the sections.

2. After joining two sections, remove the paper only from the seam allowance and press your seams open as flat as possible with a hot, dry iron.

JOIN THE SECTIONS IN THE FOLLOWING ORDER

1. Sew together sections A and C, then add section B to unit (A/C).

2. Now, add section D and then section E to unit (A/C/B), as well as section I. Set aside.

3. Sew together sections G and F and add section H to unit (G/F).

4. Next, join unit (A/C/B/D/E/I) and unit (G/F/H). Set aside.

5. Sew together sections J and K, then add section L to unit (J/K). Set aside.

6. Sew together sections N and O, then add section P to unit (N/O).

7. Now, add section Q to unit (N/O/P), followed by section M.

8. Join unit (J/K/L) and unit (N/O/P/Q/M).

9. To finish, piece the top and bottom halves together.

MICHAEL THE MONKEY
QUILT BLOCK SIZE: 8 X 8 INCHES (20.3 X 20.3 CM)

If you've ever been to Southeast Asia, especially visiting temple areas, then you know these cheeky little primates. Michael the Monkey is a very gentle creature, and of course he doesn't try to steal anything from you, unlike his mischievous buddies.

This pattern is for the advanced quilter, and has many small pieces.

Being precise and accurate when sewing on the lines ensures alignment of the sections. I suggest double-checking the alignment of two sections when joining them; this saves you from unpicking your seams.

FABRIC NEEDED (YARDAGE BASED ON FABRIC WIDTH 44" TO 45" [112 TO 115 CM]):

- Yellow: ¼ yard (1 fat quarter) (46 x 56 cm)
- Dark brown: ⅛ yard (1 fat eighth) (23 x 56 cm)
- Medium brown: about 10" x 10" (26 x 26 cm)
- Light brown: about 10" x 10" (26 x 26 cm)
- Beige: about 10" x 10" (26 x 26 cm)
- Pink: about 5" x 5" (13 x 13 cm) (just the lips)
- White: about 5" x 5" (13 x 13 cm)
- Black: about 2" x 2" (5 x 5 cm) (just the eyes)

ASSEMBLY INSTRUCTIONS

1. Trace or copy your templates (pages 100–103) onto your paper, then cut them out. Sew each section as described in "Foundation Paper Piecing Made Easy" (page 13). When joining sections, refer to the numbered overview (page 99).

2. After joining two sections, remove the paper only from the seam allowance and press the seams open with a hot, dry iron.

JOIN THE SECTIONS IN THE FOLLOWING ORDER

1. Sew together sections A and C. Add sections E and then F to unit (A/C), followed by sections G and H. Set aside.

2. Sew together sections B and D, then add sections I and J to unit (B/D), followed by sections K and L. Set aside.

3. Sew together sections T and U, then add section Q to unit (T/U).

4. Sew together sections P and O, add section N to unit (P/O) and then section M.

5. Join unit (T/U/Q) and unit (P/O/N/M).

6. Sew together sections S and V, then add section R to unit (S/V), followed by section W.

7. Join unit (A/C/E/F/G/H) and unit (T/U/Q/P/O/N/M). Set aside.

8. Join unit (B/D/I/J/K/L) and unit (S/V/R/W).

9. To finish, piece the two halves of the monkey together.

ELISA THE ELEPHANT

QUILT BLOCK SIZE: 8 X 8 INCHES (20.3 X 20.3 CM)

One of my favorite animals is the elephant. Whether Asian or African, both kinds are absolutely stunning and nothing short of amazing. Elisa the Elephant is from India and thus is smaller than her fellow elephants in Africa. She will be decorated for the elephant festival of Jaipur. Elephants symbolize royalty according to the traditions of Rajasthan. Doesn't Elisa look like a real queen?

This quilt block gives you so many options. How about sewing it onto a bag, a pillowcase or wall hanging in a small frame? An elephant embellishes almost everything.

As you can see, this pattern has some small pieces, so being accurate when sewing your sections ensures alignment when joining the sections.

FABRIC NEEDED (YARDAGE BASED ON FABRIC WIDTH 44" TO 45" [112 TO 115 CM]):

- Orange: ¼ yard (1 fat quarter) (46 x 56 cm)
- Light gray: ⅛ yard (1 fat eighth) (23 x 56 cm)
- Gray: about 10" x 10" (26 x 26 cm)
- White: about 5" x 5" (13 x 13 cm) (for the tusks)
- Black: about 2" x 2" (5 x 5 cm) (just the eye)

ASSEMBLY INSTRUCTIONS

1. Start by copying or tracing the templates (pages 106–108) onto your choice of paper and cut out those templates.

2. Sew each section as described in "Foundation Paper Piecing Made Easy" (page 13). Referring to the numbered overview (page 105) of the pattern simplifies the assembly of the sections.

3. Remove the paper of the seam allowance only after stitching two sections together. It makes it easier to press the seams nice and flat with a hot, dry iron.

JOIN THE SECTIONS IN THE FOLLOWING ORDER

1. Sew together sections A and B, then add section C to unit (A/B).

2. Next, sew section D to unit (A/B/C).

3. Then, add section E to unit (A/B/C/D) and then section F followed by section G. Set aside.

4. Sew together sections I and H. Set aside.

5. Sew together sections N and O.

6. Sew together sections J and K, then add section L to unit (J/K).

7. Now, join units (N/O) and (J/K/L) and add unit (I/H), then add section M to unit (N/O/J/K/L/I/H).

8. Finally, piece the head of the elephant to the body and add section P at the bottom.

COCO THE COCKATOO

QUILT BLOCK SIZE: 8 X 8 INCHES (20.3 X 20.3 CM)

Isn't Coco just the most stylish creature? Just like her famous namesake from Paris, she enjoys her freedom, flying from one tree to the next and watching jungle life go by.

This cockatoo block would look stunning on a cosmetic pouch or summer bag. It will also make a wonderful pillowcase and give your room a sunny, beachy, tropical look.

This pattern is for the advanced quilter, since it has small pieces that require careful precision. Sewing accurately on your lines ensures alignment when joining two segments.

FABRIC NEEDED (YARDAGE BASED ON FABRIC WIDTH 44" TO 45" [112 TO 115 CM]):

- Green: ¼ yard (1 fat quarter) (46 x 56 cm)
- White: ⅛ yard (1 fat eighth) (23 x 56 cm)
- Gray white: about 5" x 5" (13 x 13 cm)
- Light gray: about 5" x 5" (13 x 13 cm)
- Eggshell: about 5" x 5" (13 x 13 cm)
- Bright yellow: about 5" x 5" (13 x 13 cm)
- Light yellow: about 5" x 5" (13 x 13 cm)
- Black: about 5" x 5" (13 x 13 cm) (just the beak and the eye)
- Dark gray: about 5" x 5" (13 x 13 cm)

ASSEMBLY INSTRUCTIONS

1. Before you can sew this beauty, copy or trace the pattern templates (pages 111–113) onto your choice of paper and cut out those templates.

2. Sew each section as described in "Foundation Paper Piecing Made Easy" (page 13). Always refer to the numbered overview (page 110) when assembling the sections.

3. After joining two sections, remove the paper only from the seam allowance and press your seams open as flat as possible with a dry, hot iron.

JOIN THE SECTIONS IN THE FOLLOWING ORDER

1. Sew together sections A, B and C.

2. Sew together sections E and D.

3. Now, join units (A/B/C) and (E/D) and add section F to unit (A/B/C/E/D). Set aside.

4. Sew together sections I and J, then add section K to unit (I/J), followed by sections G and H. Set aside.

5. Sew together sections M and L, then add section O to unit (M/L), followed by sections N and P.

6. Now, join the legs unit (M/L/O/N/P) with the body unit (I/J/K/G/H).

7. To finish, piece the head and body units together.

TONI THE TOUCAN

QUILT BLOCK SIZE: 8 X 8 INCHES (20.3 X 20.3 CM)

Toni the Toucan lives in the luscious green jungle, like her best friend Coco the Cockatoo (page 81). She is highly social and loves hanging out with her friends. She can often be found in a large group of 20 or more birds.

Toni the Toucan would look stunning on a pillowcase, table runner or cosmetic or beach bag. This pattern perfectly complements the Coco the Cockatoo pattern.

Both of these quilt blocks are ideal to give your home décor and accessories a tropical feel.

FABRIC NEEDED (YARDAGE BASED ON FABRIC WIDTH 44" TO 45" [112 TO 115 CM]):

- Orange: ¼ yard (1 fat quarter) (46 x 56 cm)
- Black: ⅛ yard (1 fat eighth) (23 x 56 cm)
- White: about 8" x 8" (20 x 20 cm)
- Dark pink: about 5" x 5" (13 x 13 cm)
- Dark yellow: about 5" x 5" (13 x 13 cm)
- Yellow: about 5" x 5" (13 x 13 cm)
- Blue: about 2" x 2" (5 x 5 cm) (just the eye)

ASSEMBLY INSTRUCTIONS

1. Start by tracing or copying the templates (pages 116–118) onto your choice of paper, and cut out those templates. Then sew each section as described in "Foundation Paper Piecing Made Easy" (page 13). Refer to the numbered overview (page 115) as you assemble the sections.

2. After joining two sections, remove the paper only from the seam allowance and press the seams open and as flat as possible with a hot, dry iron.

JOIN THE SECTIONS IN THE FOLLOWING ORDER

1. Sew together sections A and B.

2. Sew together sections C and D and add section E to unit (C/D).

3. Join units (A/B) and (C/D/E) and set aside.

4. Sew together sections G and F; add section H to unit (G/F) and then section I.

5. Sew together sections M and K. Add section N to unit (M/K), then add section L.

6. Next, add section O to unit (M/K/N/L) at the bottom and section J at the top.

7. Now, add section P to unit (M/K/N/L/O/J).

8. Join units (M/K/N/L/O/J/P) and (G/F/H/I).

9. Finish by joining the head unit with the body unit of the toucan.

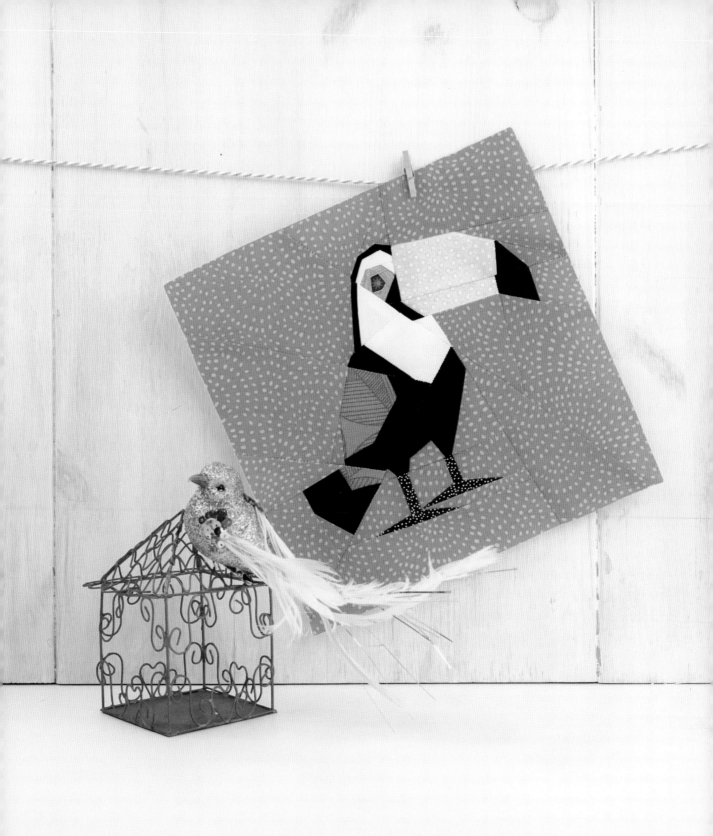

→ ZOE THE ZEBRA ←
QUILT BLOCK SIZE: 8 X 8 INCHES (20.3 X 20.3 CM)

Zoe the Zebra is like a horse, only prettier. She lives in the grasslands, plains or the savannas of Africa. Zoe lives in a small herd and she has extremely good hearing and vision. Her stripes usually help her blend in, though not if they're pink!

I didn't make Zoe in her traditional black and white colors so I could show how fun these patterns can be if you think outside the box. This would make a stunning Andy Warhol–like wall hanging with four differently colored zebras.

I say this all the time throughout this book: Being precise and sewing right on the pattern line makes assembly of the sections so much easier and keeps you from unpicking your seams and getting frustrated.

FABRIC NEEDED (YARDAGE BASED ON FABRIC WIDTH 44" TO 45" [112 TO 115 CM]):

- Beige: ¼ yard (1 fat quarter) (46 x 56 cm)
- Pink: ⅛ yard (1 fat eighth) (23 x 56 cm)
- Orange: about 5" x 5" (13 x 13 cm)
- Black: about 5" x 5" (13 x 13 cm)

ASSEMBLY INSTRUCTIONS

1. The first step for this pattern is tracing or copying the templates (pages 121–124) onto your choice of paper and cutting out those templates. Then, sew each section as described in "Foundation Paper Piecing Made Easy" (page 13). Always refer to the numbered overview (page 120) when assembling the sections.

2. After joining two sections, remove the paper only from the seam allowance and press your seams open as flat as possible with a hot, dry iron.

JOIN THE SECTIONS IN THE FOLLOWING ORDER

1. Sew together sections K and J, then add section I to unit (K/J). Set aside.

2. Sew together sections H and G.

3. Sew together sections E and F and add to unit (H/G).

4. Next add section B to unit (H/G/E/F).

5. Sew together sections D and C and add unit (D/C) to unit (H/G/E/F/B).

6. Now, add section L at the bottom of unit (H/G/E/F/B/D/C) and section A at the top.

7. To finish, piece the top and bottom halves together.

KARLA THE KANGAROO

QUILT BLOCK SIZE: 8 X 8 INCHES (20.3 X 20.3 CM)

As we all know, Karla the Kangaroo is from Australia, but some of her family lives on the Galapagos Islands. She lives in a large group of other kangaroos called a mob, but she also enjoys her solitude. She can jump an enormous distance and at an impressive speed as well.

This pattern is for the intermediate quilter. It would look great on a backpack, or travel or cosmetic pouch, as well as on a mini quilt or fabric basket for your child's stuffed animals.

FABRIC NEEDED (YARDAGE BASED ON FABRIC WIDTH 44" TO 45" [112 TO 115 CM]):

- Dark red: ¼ yard (1 fat quarter) (46 x 56 cm)
- Medium brown: ⅛ yard (1 fat eighth) (23 x 56 cm)
- Light brown: about 10" x 10" (26 x 26 cm)
- Sand: about 5" x 5" (13 x 13 cm)
- Pink: about 2" x 2" (5 x 5 cm) (just the lips)
- Black: about 2" x 2" (5 x 5 cm) (just the eye)

ASSEMBLY INSTRUCTIONS

1. Before you start sewing this pattern, copy or trace the templates (pages 127–129) onto the paper of your choice and cut out the templates. Then, sew each section as described in "Foundation Paper Piecing Made Easy" (page 13). Please refer to the numbered overview (page 126) as you assemble the sections.

2. Remove the paper from the seam allowance only after joining two sections. Then, press the seams open as flat as possible with a hot, dry iron. This gives you nice crisp and flat seams.

JOIN THE SECTIONS IN THE FOLLOWING ORDER

1. Sew together sections B and C, then add section A to unit (B/C), followed by section D.

2. Sew together sections E and F. Join unit (E/F) with unit (B/C/A/D).

3. Sew together sections G and H and add section I to unit (G/H). Join unit (G/H/I) with the head unit (B/C/A/D/E/F).

4. Sew together sections K and J.

5. Sew together sections L and M, then add unit (L/M) to unit (K/J).

6. Now, add section N to unit (K/J/L/M), followed by section O and then section P.

7. To finish, piece the front and body halves together.

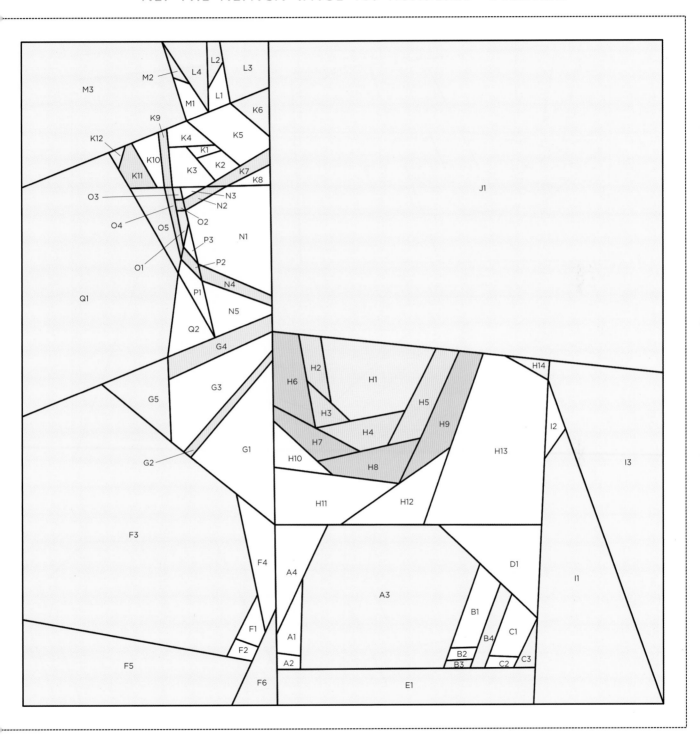

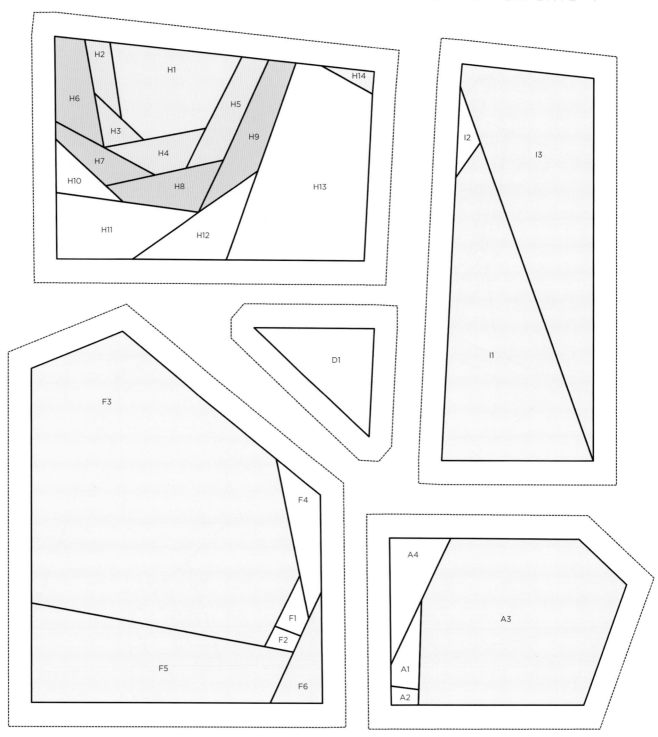

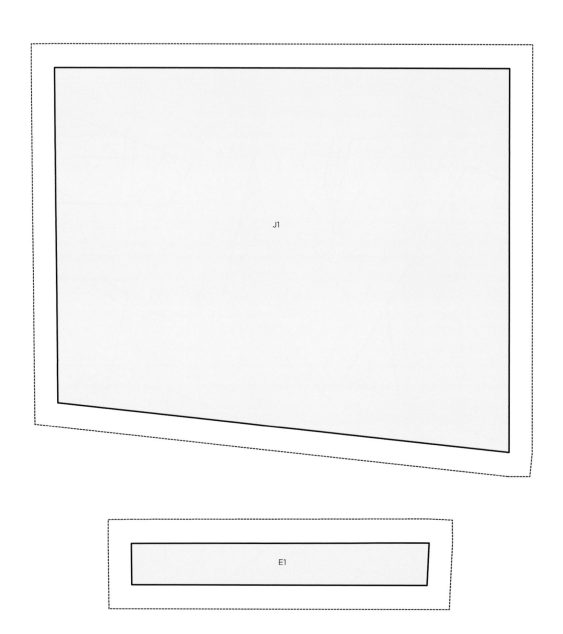

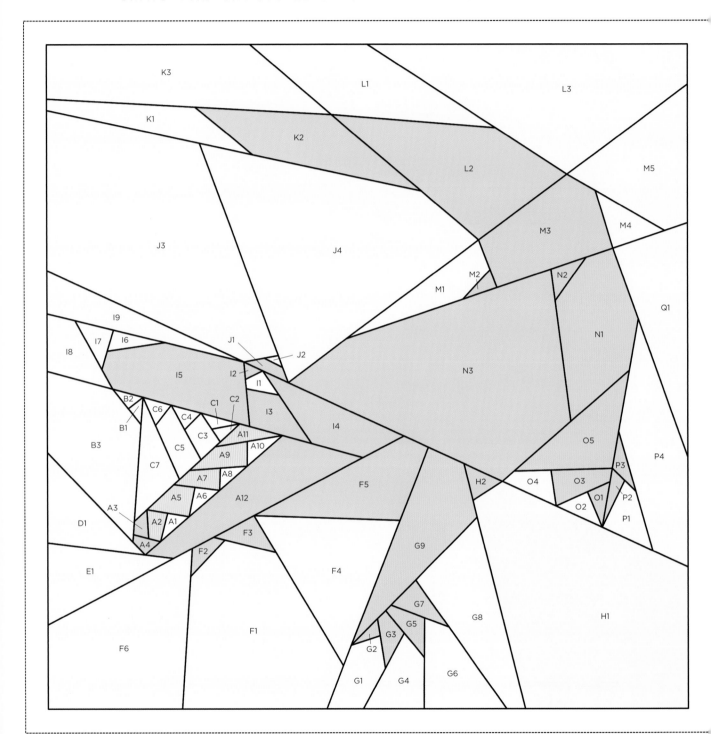

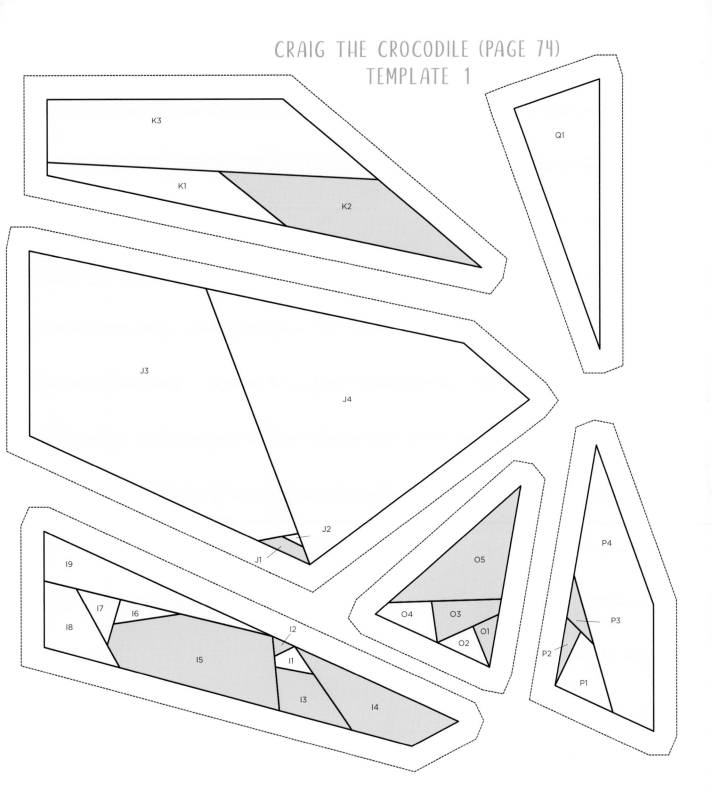

CRAIG THE CROCODILE (PAGE 74)
TEMPLATE 1

K3
K1
K2
Q1
J3
J4
J2
J1
I9
I7
I6
I8
I2
I5
I1
I3
I4
O5
O4
O3
O2
O1
P4
P3
P2
P1

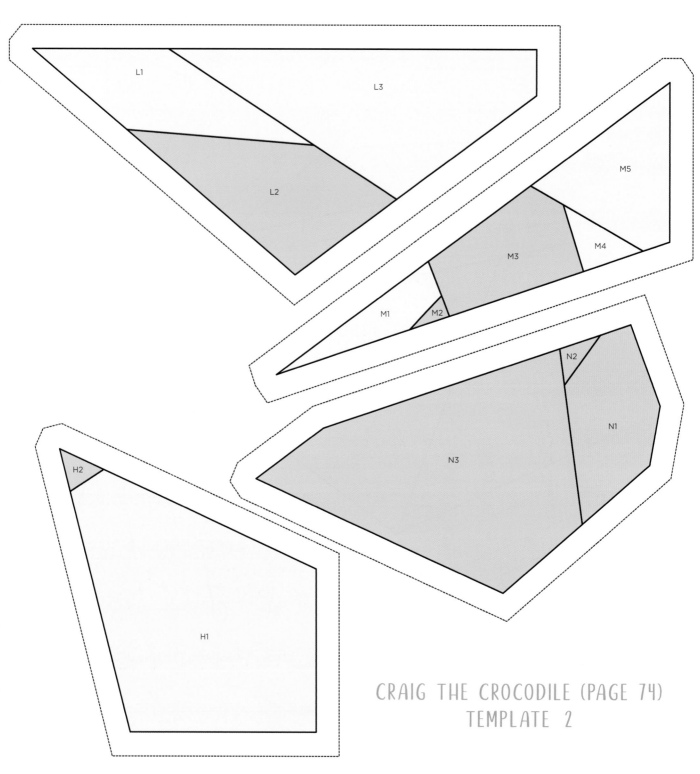

CRAIG THE CROCODILE (PAGE 74)
TEMPLATE 2

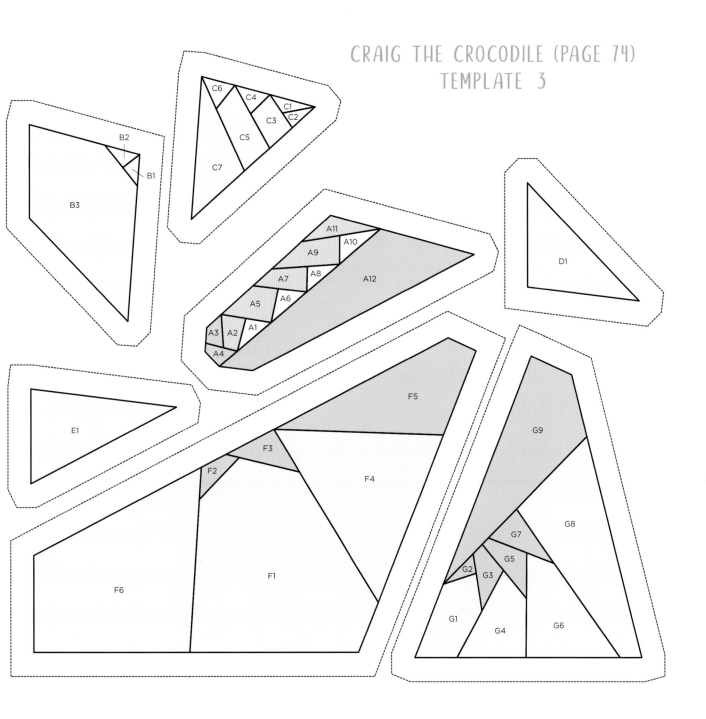

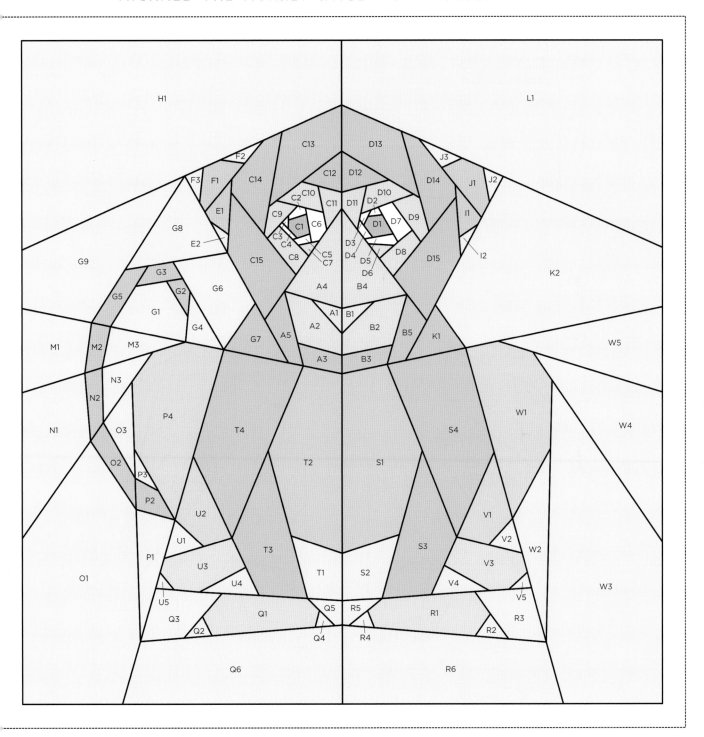

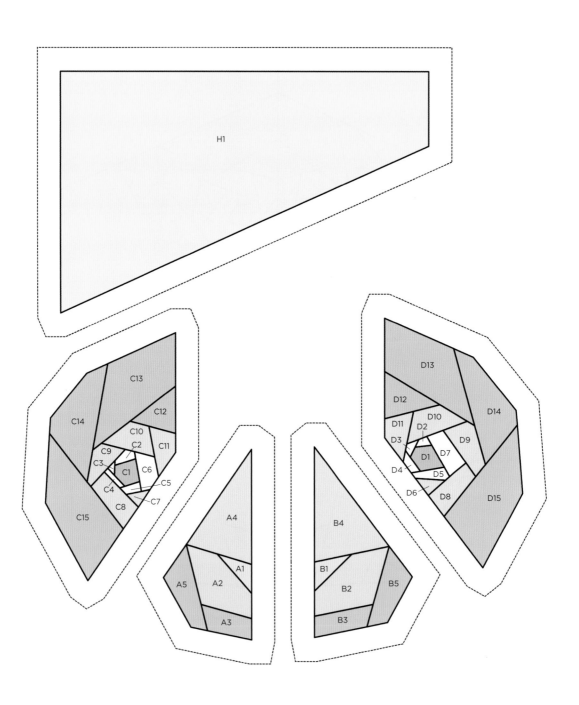

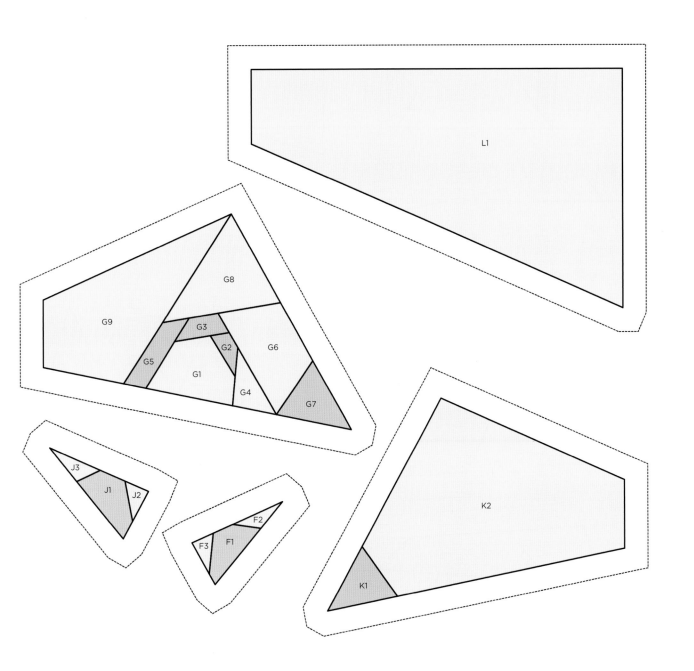

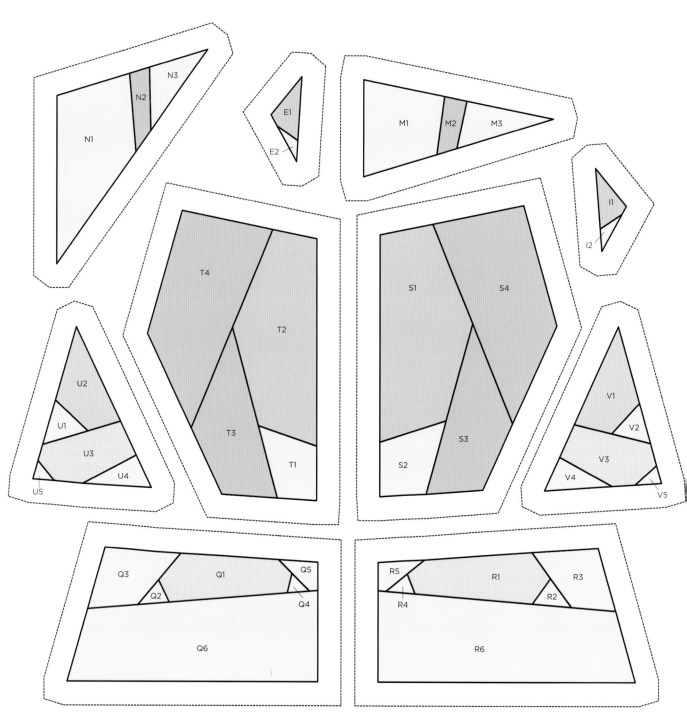

P4

P3

P2

P1

O3

O2

O1

W5

W1

W4

W2

W3

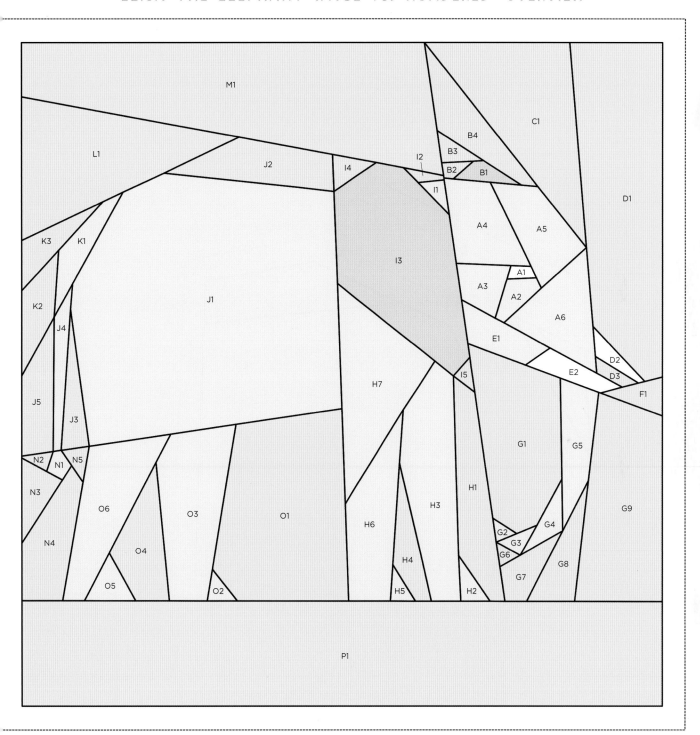

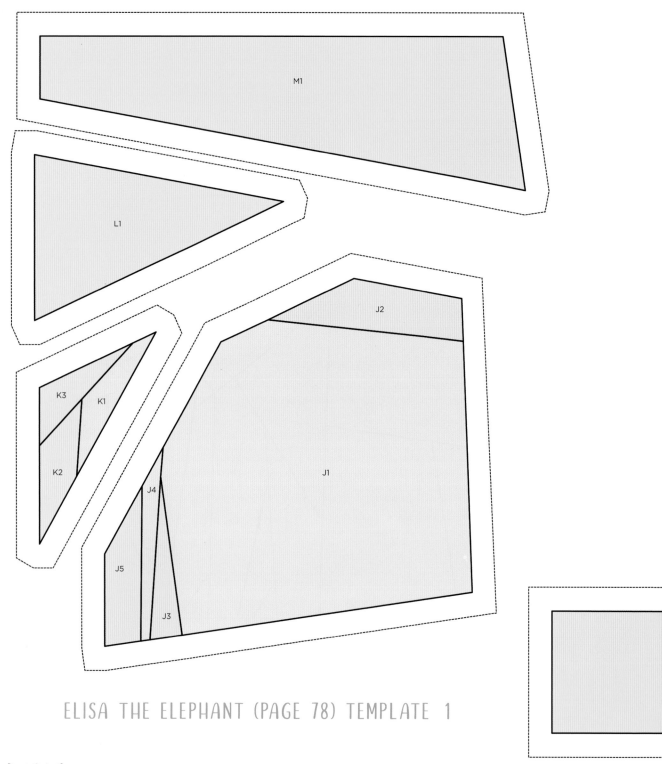

ELISA THE ELEPHANT (PAGE 78) TEMPLATE 1

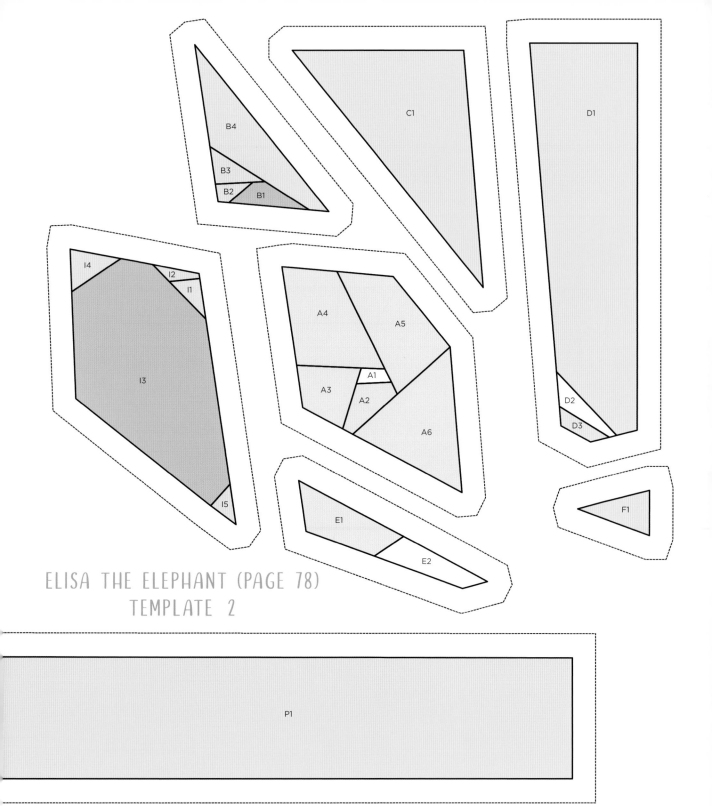

ELISA THE ELEPHANT (PAGE 78)
TEMPLATE 2

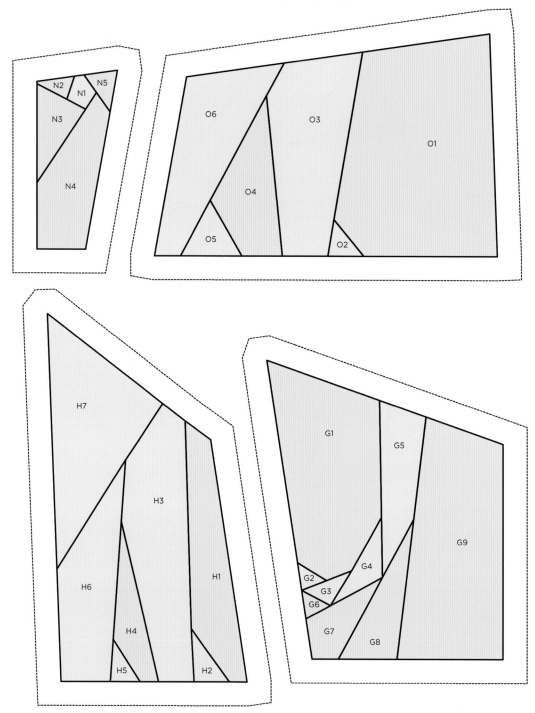

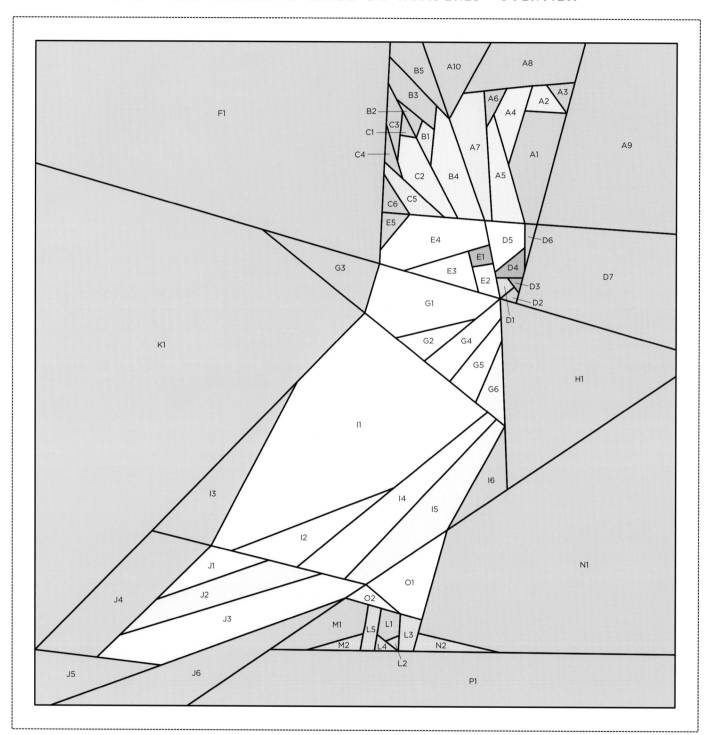

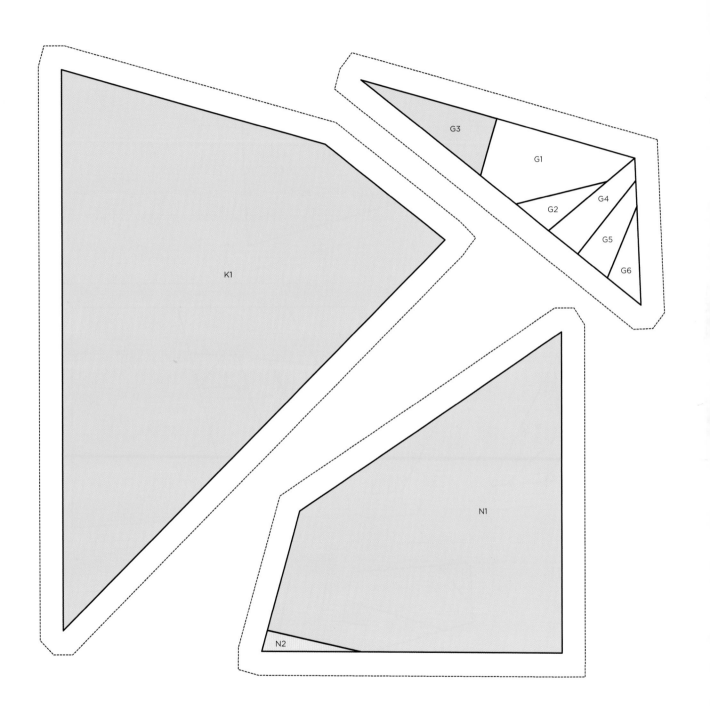

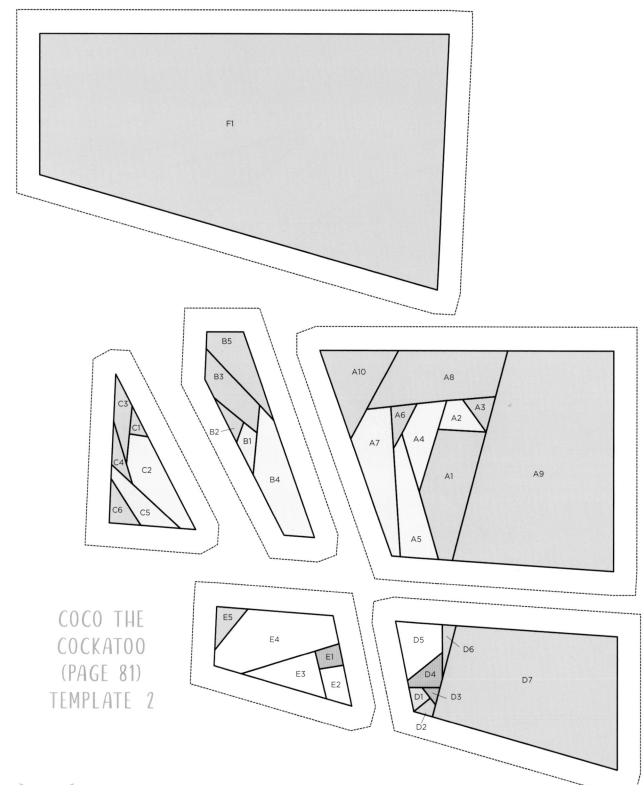

COCO THE
COCKATOO
(PAGE 81)
TEMPLATE 2

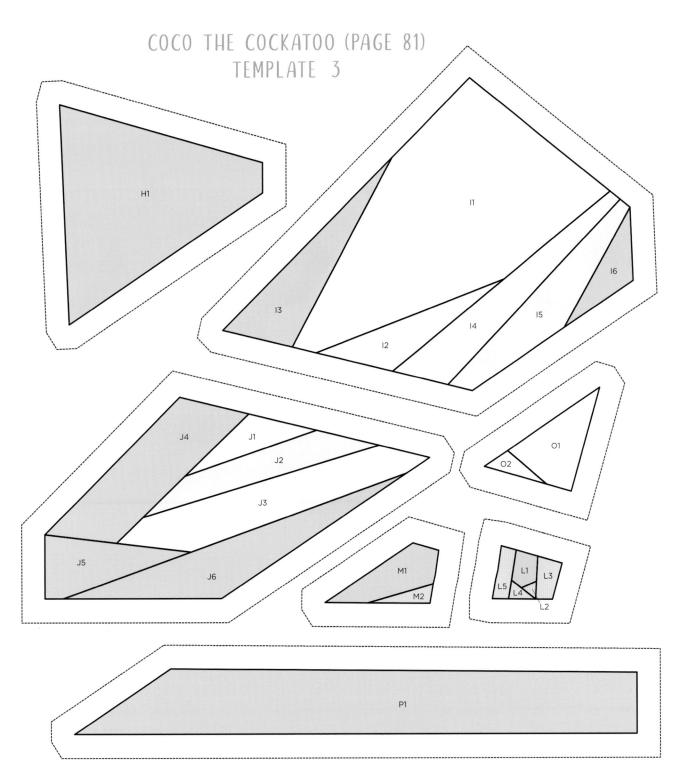

COCO THE COCKATOO (PAGE 81)
TEMPLATE 3

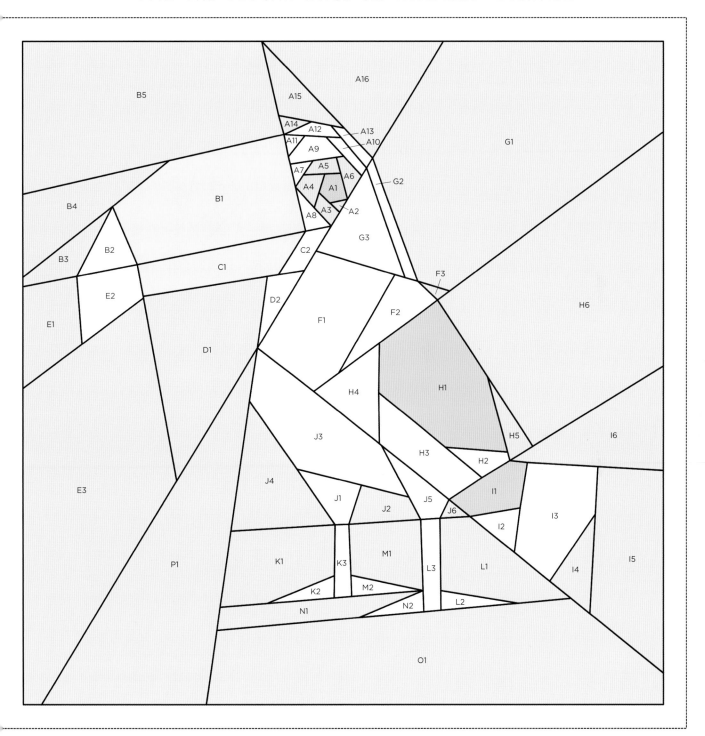

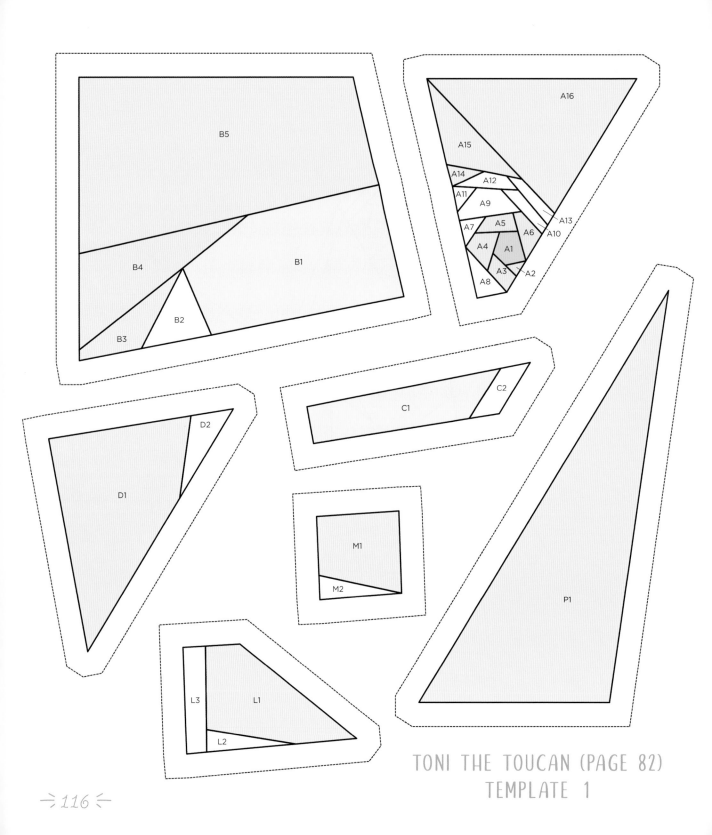

TONI THE TOUCAN (PAGE 82)
TEMPLATE 1

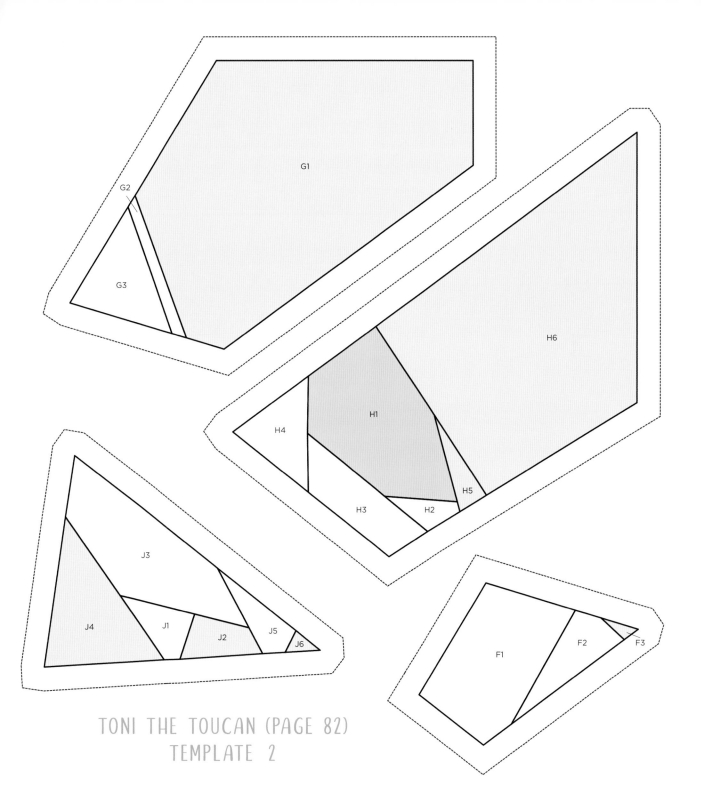

TONI THE TOUCAN (PAGE 82)
TEMPLATE 2

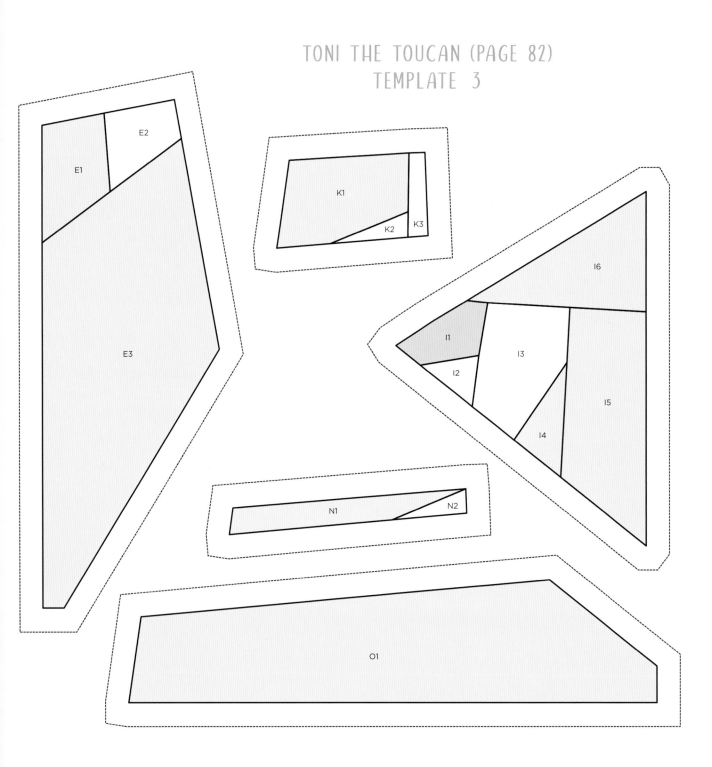

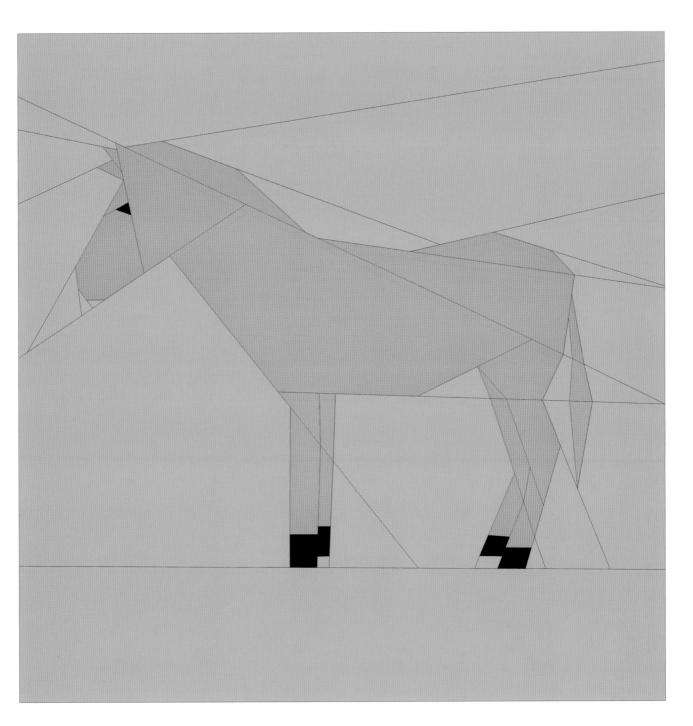

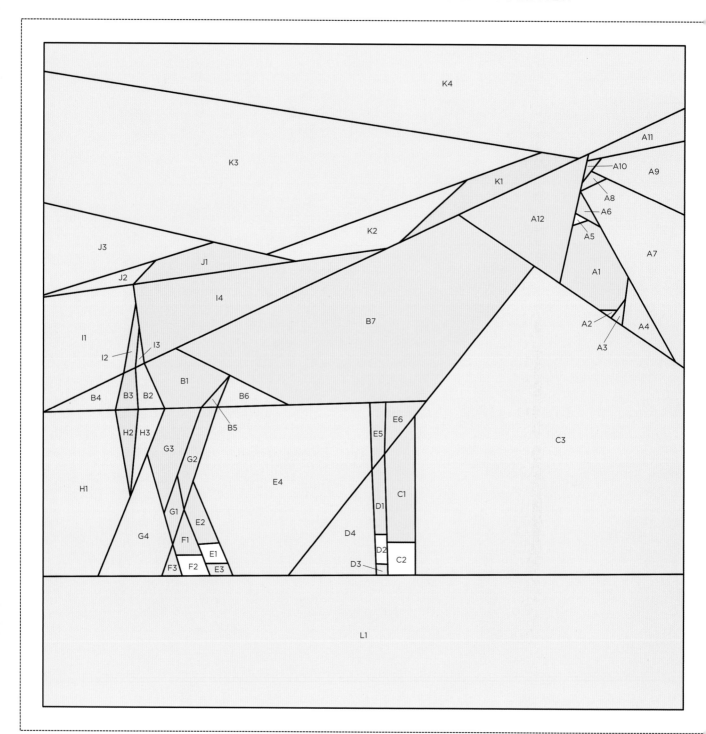

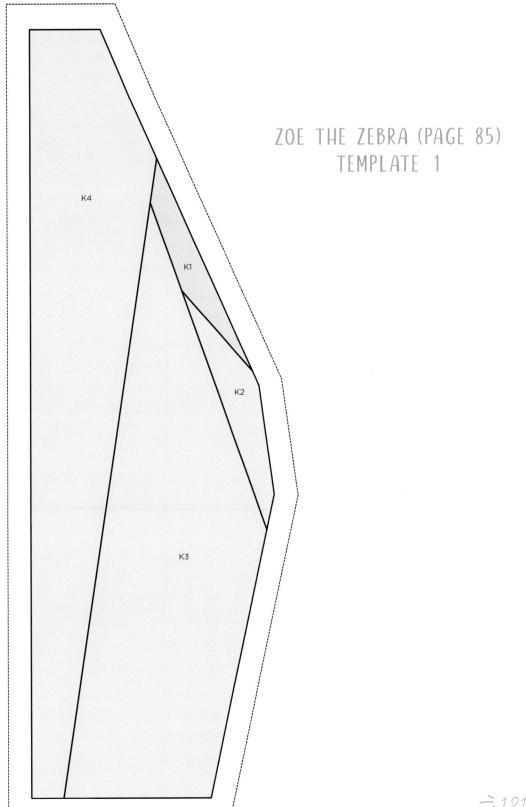

ZOE THE ZEBRA (PAGE 85)
TEMPLATE 1

K4

K1

K2

K3

ZOE THE ZEBRA (PAGE 85)
TEMPLATE 2

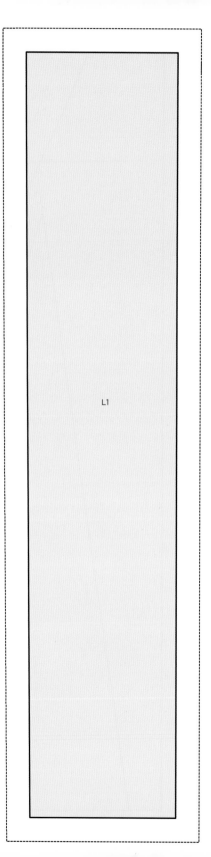

L1

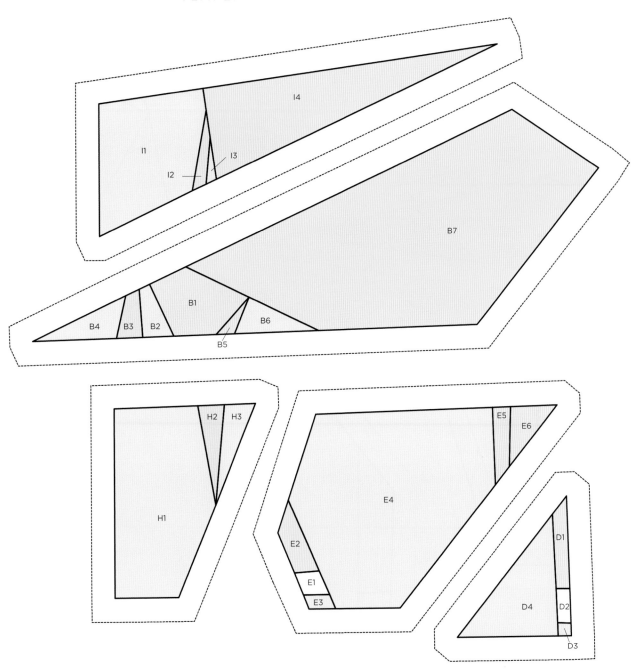

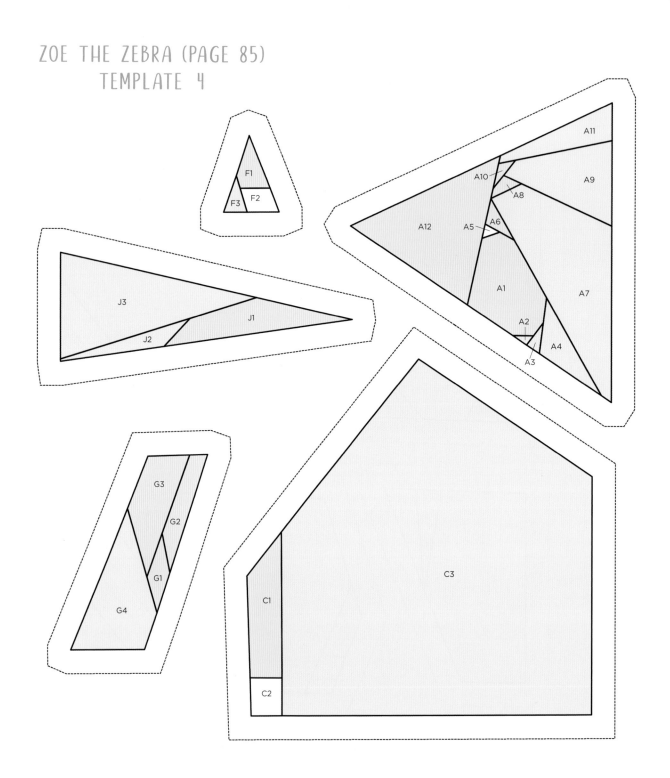

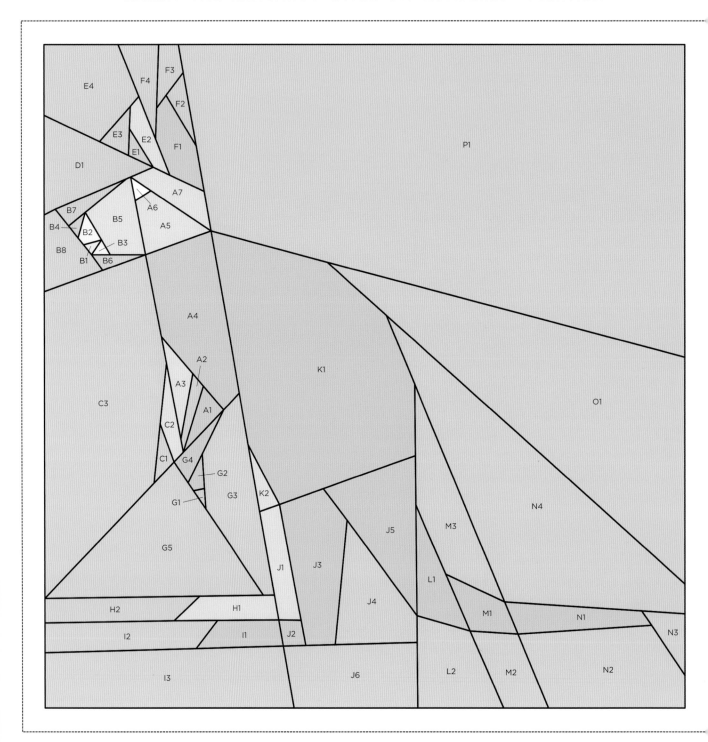

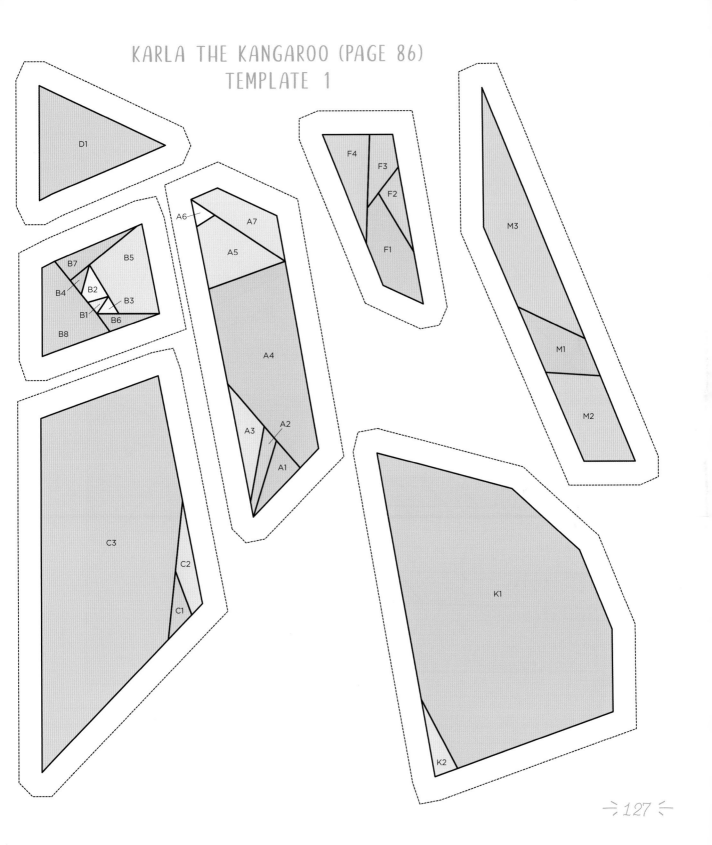

KARLA THE KANGAROO (PAGE 86)
TEMPLATE 1

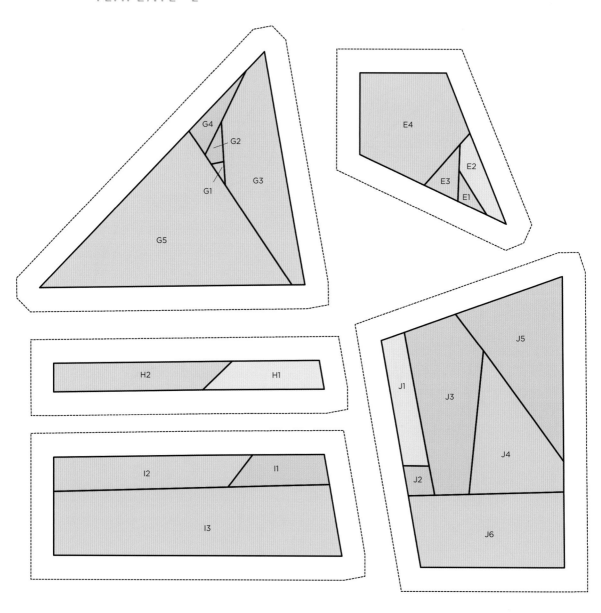

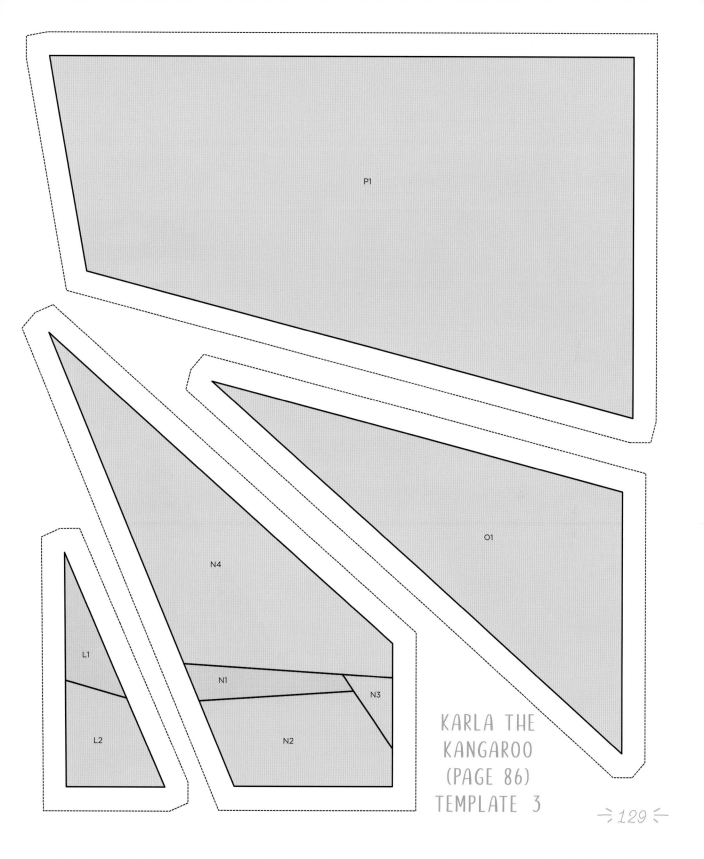

KARLA THE
KANGAROO
(PAGE 86)
TEMPLATE 3

Magnificent Ocean Creatures

Living on the Canadian West Coast for a long time gave me plenty of opportunities to witness these fantastic ocean creatures in their natural habitat. Being able to watch orcas up close, swimming in a pod of up to 30 whales along the Vancouver coastline, emerging from the ocean and breaching clear of the water, is amazing.

Dolphins and sea lions populate the coast all the way down to Mexico. Discovering pods of dolphins or colonies of sea lions isn't a rare occurrence. Huge sea lion colonies can often be seen on seaside rocks along the North American West Coast.

With these stunning patterns, you can easily create an ocean vibe for your home. Add some coastal décor to your living room with pillowcases featuring Dotty the Dolphin (page 133), Olly the Orca (page 141) or Sasha the Sea Lion (page 138).

Sally the Seahorse (page 137) would look stunning on a beach bag or bikini pouch. Of course, a whole quilt with all the magnificent ocean creatures would just be the perfect addition to your coastal interior.

Grab your favorite oceanic blue fabric scraps and off we go. . . .

DOTTY THE DOLPHIN

QUILT BLOCK SIZE: 8 X 8 INCHES (20.3 X 20.3 CM)

Swimming with dolphins is an amazing adventure. Experiencing these gentle creatures up close is something you'll never forget. Dotty the Dolphin is a very agile mammal and interacts joyfully with children on boating trips.

This pattern is fairly simple and would be manageable for beginners. Keep in mind that precision, nonetheless, is very important—the more accurately you sew, the easier the assembly of the sections will be.

FABRIC NEEDED (YARDAGE BASED ON FABRIC WIDTH 44" TO 45" [112 TO 115 CM]):

- Baby blue: ¼ yard (1 fat quarter) (46 x 56 cm)
- Royal blue: ⅛ yard (1 fat eighth) (23 x 56 cm)
- Gray blue: about 5" x 5" (13 x 13 cm)
- Black: about 2" x 2" (5 x 5 cm) (just the eye)

ASSEMBLY INSTRUCTIONS

1. Begin by copying or tracing the pattern templates (pages 144-146) onto your choice of paper, then cut out these templates along the dotted line. Next, sew each section as described in "Foundation Paper Piecing Made Easy" (page 13). Referring to the numbered overview (page 143) as you assemble the sections helps you tremendously.

2. After joining two sections, remove the paper only from the seam allowance and press your seams open as flat as possible with a hot, dry iron.

JOIN THE SECTIONS IN THE FOLLOWING ORDER

1. Sew together sections A and B.

2. Sew together sections F and E, then add section G to unit (F/E).

3. Now, join unit (F/E/G) with unit (A/B). Set aside.

4. Sew together sections C and D. Set aside.

5. Sew together sections H and I, then add sections J, K and L to unit (H/I), in that order.

6. Join unit (H/I/J/K/L) with unit (C/D).

7. To finish, piece the two dolphin halves together.

TULA THE TURTLE

QUILT BLOCK SIZE: 8 X 8 INCHES (20.3 X 20.3 CM)

Tula is actually a sea turtle. She lives in almost every ocean throughout the world but nests only on tropical beaches. How convenient, right? This pattern captures Tula swimming in the ocean in her full beauty.

This is a pattern for the intermediate quilter and looks really fun in all sorts of color combinations. Can't you just picture a couple of turtle pillows on a wooden bench or your living room couch?

FABRIC NEEDED (YARDAGE BASED ON FABRIC WIDTH 44" TO 45" [112 TO 115 CM]):

- Blue: ¼ yard (1 fat quarter) (46 x 56 cm)
- Pink: about 10" x 10" (26 x 26 cm)
- Orange: about 10" x 10" (26 x 26 cm)
- Beige: about 10" x 10" (26 x 26 cm)
- Black: about 2" x 2" (5 x 5 cm) (just the eye)

ASSEMBLY INSTRUCTIONS

1. Copy or trace the pattern templates (pages 149–151) and cut out those templates.

2. Sew each section as described in "Foundation Paper Piecing Made Easy" (page 13). Refer to the numbered overview (page 148) for assembly of your sections.

3. When you have joined two sections, remove the paper only from the seam allowance and press your seams open as flat as possible with a hot, dry iron.

JOIN THE SECTIONS IN THE FOLLOWING ORDER

1. Sew together sections A and B.

2. Sew together sections D and E.

3. Sew together sections H, G and F, then add unit (H/G/F) to unit (D/E).

4. Next, add section C on top of unit (D/E/H/G/F) and unit (A/B) at the front to make the top part of the turtle. Set aside.

5. Sew together sections K and M, then add section L to unit (K/M).

6. Sew together sections O and N, then add unit (O/N) to unit (K/M/L).

7. Now, add section J to unit (K/M/L/O/N), followed by section I, to make the bottom half of the turtle.

8. To finish, piece the top and bottom halves together.

SALLY THE SEAHORSE

QUILT BLOCK SIZE: 8 X 8 INCHES (20.3 X 20.3 CM)

Sally the Seahorse is a fascinating little creature. Sally lives with her mate for life, just like swans do. She can change her color very quickly to match her surroundings; sometimes she's even bright red.

I made this pattern in a couple of colors to show how pretty she is in every hue. These cute little seahorses just ask for all sorts of colorways.

Anything from a pillowcase to a mini-quilt, placemats or a fun little beach pouch would look absolutely adorable with this pattern. This quilt block makes it easy to give your home or accessories a coastal look.

FABRIC NEEDED (YARDAGE BASED ON FABRIC WIDTH 44" TO 45" [112 TO 115 CM]):

- Dark blue: ¼ yard (1 fat quarter) (46 x 56 cm)
- Light pink: ⅛ yard (1 fat eighth) (23 x 56 cm)
- Magenta: about 10" x 10" (26 x 26 cm)
- Pink: about 5" x 5" (13 x 13 cm)
- Black: about 2" x 2" (5 x 5 cm) (just the eye)

ASSEMBLY INSTRUCTIONS

1. Start by tracing or copying the templates (pages 154–156) onto your choice of paper, then cut out those templates. Now, sew each section as described in "Foundation Paper Piecing Made Easy" (page 13). When joining the sections, refer to the numbered overview (page 153).

2. After stitching two sections together, remove the paper only from the seam allowance and press your seams open as flat as possible with a hot, dry iron.

JOIN THE SECTIONS IN THE FOLLOWING ORDER

1. Sew together sections A and E, then add section B to unit (A/E), followed by section C and then section D. Set aside.

2. Sew together sections F and G.

3. Sew together sections I and H.

4. Sew together sections K and J, then add unit (K/J) to unit (I/H).

5. Join unit (F/G) with unit (I/H/K/J).

6. To finish, piece the head and body halves together.

SASHA THE SEA LION

QUILT BLOCK SIZE: 8 X 8 INCHES (20.3 X 20.3 CM)

Sasha the Sea Lion is probably one of the most adorable creatures the ocean has to offer. He's extremely social and intelligent and lives in a large group with other sea lions, which is very noisy at times. Sasha is a really good eater—he needs 30 pounds (almost 14 kg) of seafood a day.

This pattern captures Sasha doing exactly that: eating his favorite fish.

FABRIC NEEDED (YARDAGE BASED ON FABRIC WIDTH 44" TO 45" [112 TO 115 CM]):

- Sand: ¼ yard (1 fat quarter) (46 x 56 cm)
- Bordeaux: ⅛ yard (1 fat eighth) (23 x 56 cm)
- Blue: about 5" x 5" (13 x 13 cm)
- Black: about 2" x 2" (5 x 5 cm) (just the eye)
- Dark Bordeaux: about 5" x 5" (12 x 12 cm)

ASSEMBLY INSTRUCTIONS

1. Begin by tracing or copying the templates (pages 159–161) onto your choice of paper, then cut out the templates. Next, sew each section as described in "Foundation Paper Piecing Made Easy" (page 13). Always refer to the numbered overview (page 158) when assembling the sections.

2. After joining two sections, remove the paper only from the seam allowance and press your seams open as flat as possible with a hot, dry iron.

JOIN THE SECTIONS IN THE FOLLOWING ORDER

1. Sew together sections A and B, then add section C to unit (A/B), followed by section D. Next, add sections E, F and G to unit (A/B/C/D), in that order.

2. Sew together sections J and K. Then add section L to unit (J/K), followed by section M.

3. Add section N to unit (J/K/L/M).

4. Now, add section I to unit (J/K/L/M/N), followed by section O and then section H.

5. To finish, piece the top and bottom halves together.

→ OLLY THE ORCA ←

QUILT BLOCK SIZE: 8 X 8 INCHES (20.3 X 20.3 CM)

The Pacific Ocean is home to Olly the Orca. If you've ever been on a whale-watching cruise, you know how amazing these creatures are. It is definitely an experience you'll never forget. Olly lives with his family and friends in a pod of about 30 killer whales. Olly is a magnificent and highly social mammal that makes a wide variety of communicative sounds so that the members of his pod will recognize him even at a distance.

You can use this pattern for a variety of objects, from pillowcases, pouches and bags to backpacks and wall hangings. Of course, a whole quilt with all the ocean creatures would look especially stunning.

FABRIC NEEDED (YARDAGE BASED ON FABRIC WIDTH 44" TO 45" [112 TO 115 CM]):

- Baby blue: ¼ yard (1 fat quarter) (46 x 56 cm)
- Black: ⅛ yard (1 fat eighth) (23 x 56 cm)
- Light gray: about 2" x 2" (5 x 5 cm) (just the eye)
- White: about 10" x 10" (26 x 26 cm)

ASSEMBLY INSTRUCTIONS

1. Trace or copy the pattern templates (pages 164–166) and cut them out. Then, sew each section as described in "Foundation Paper Piecing Made Easy" (page 13). Refer to the numbered overview (page 163) when assembling the sections.

2. After you joined two sections, remove the paper only from the seam allowance and press your seams open as flat as possible with a hot, dry iron.

JOIN THE SECTIONS IN THE FOLLOWING ORDER

1. Sew together sections A and B, then add sections C, D and E to unit (A/B), in that order. Set aside.

2. Sew together sections M and L.

3. Sew together sections K and I. Add section H to unit (K/I), then section J.

4. Now, join unit (K/I/H/J) with unit (M/L) and set aside.

5. Sew together sections G and F and join unit (G/F) with the tail unit of the orca (K/I/H/J/M/L).

6. To finish, piece the top and bottom halves together.

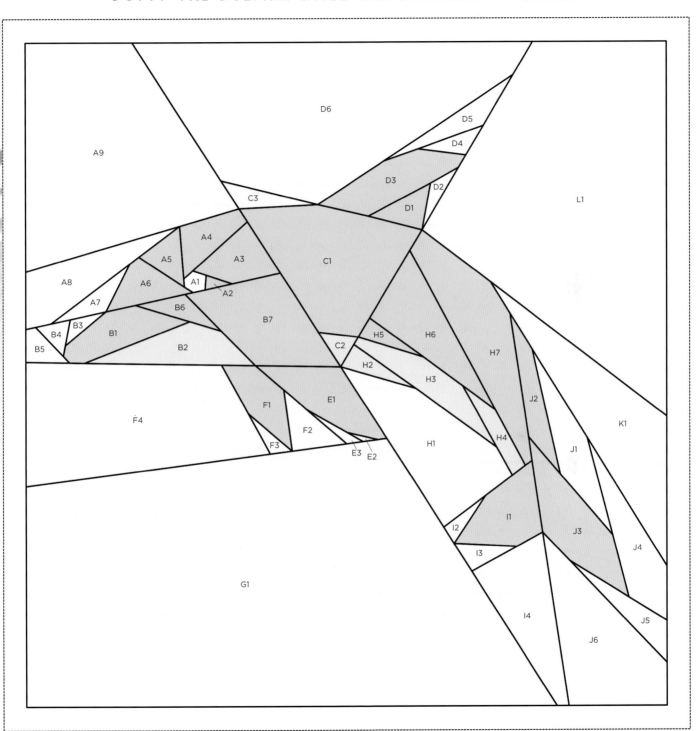

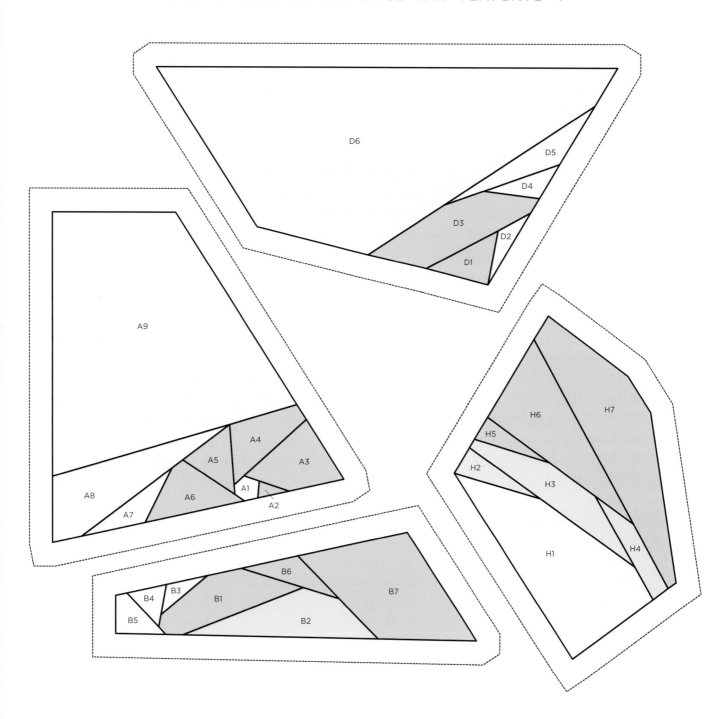

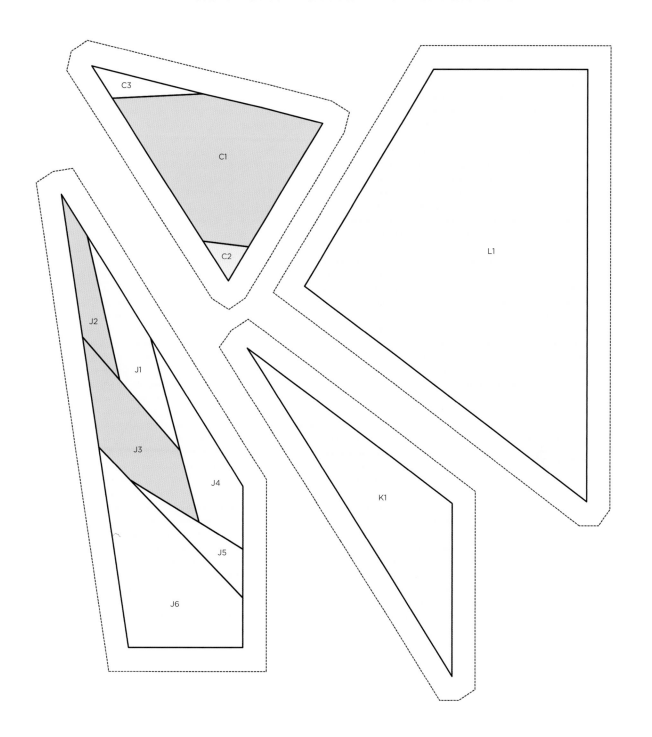

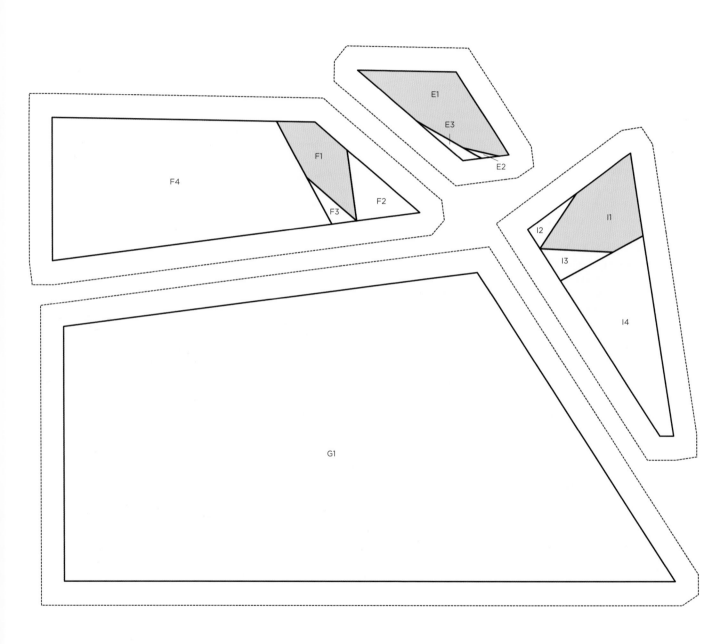

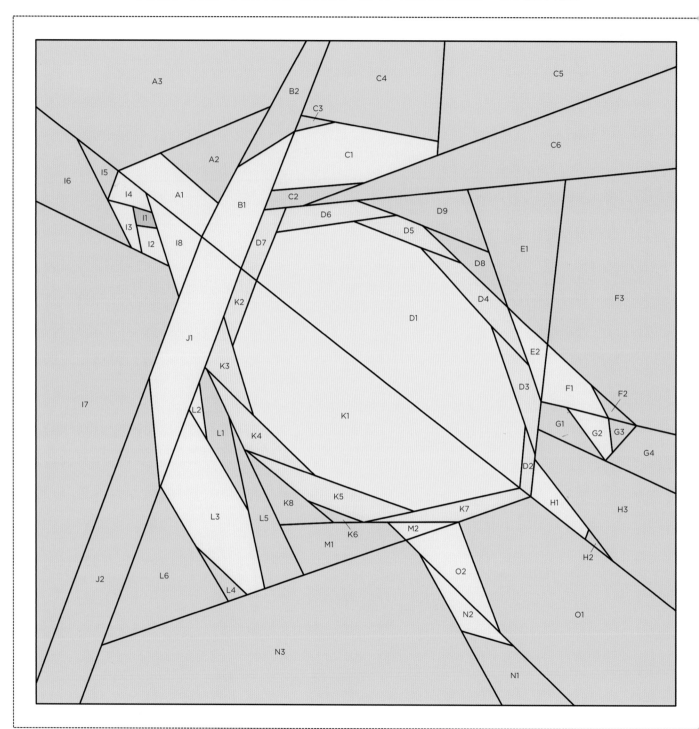

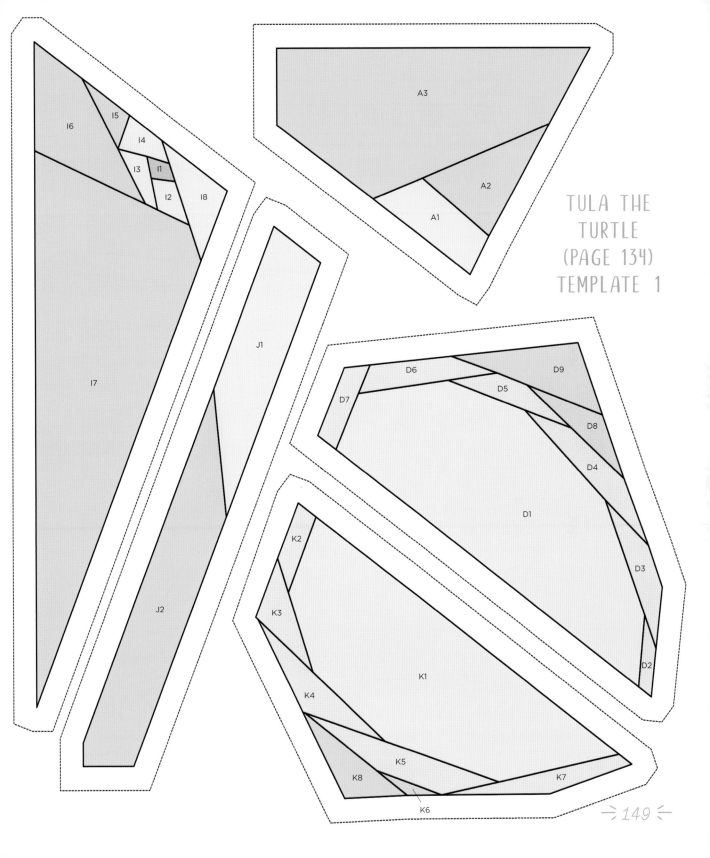

TULA THE
TURTLE
(PAGE 134)
TEMPLATE 1

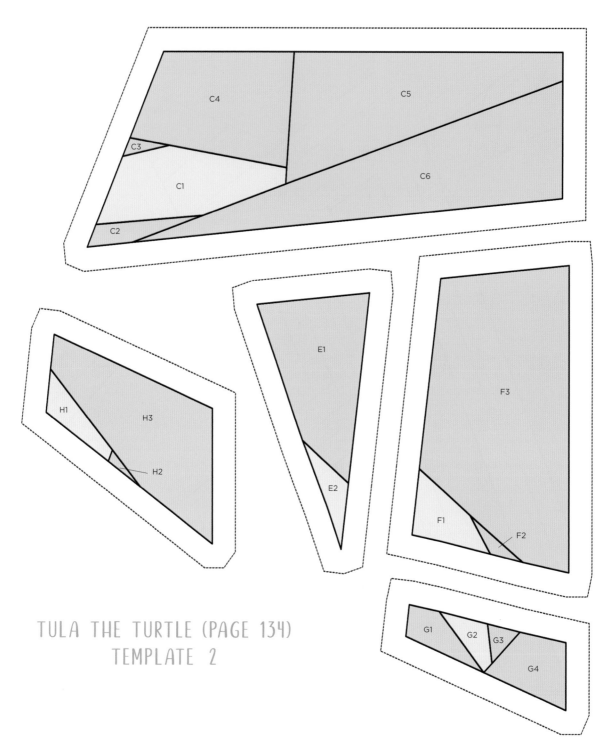

TULA THE TURTLE (PAGE 134)
TEMPLATE 2

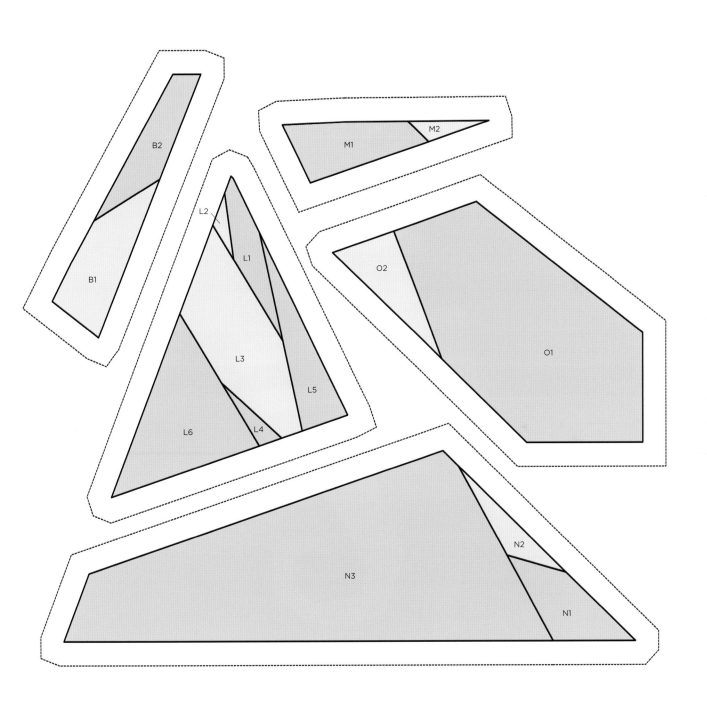

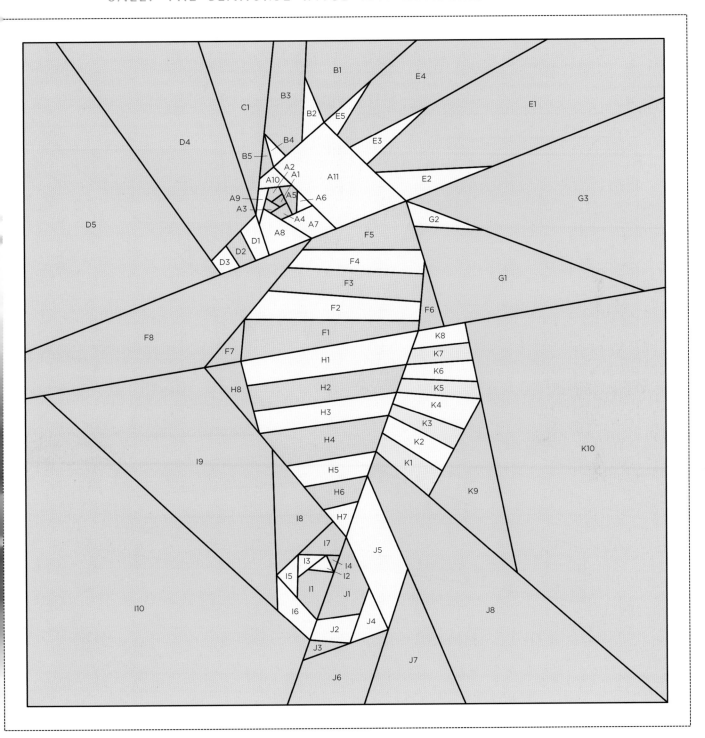

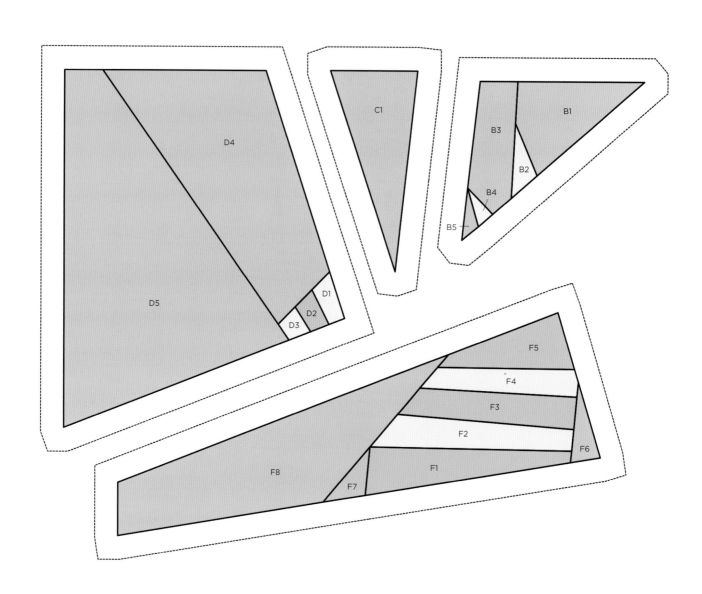

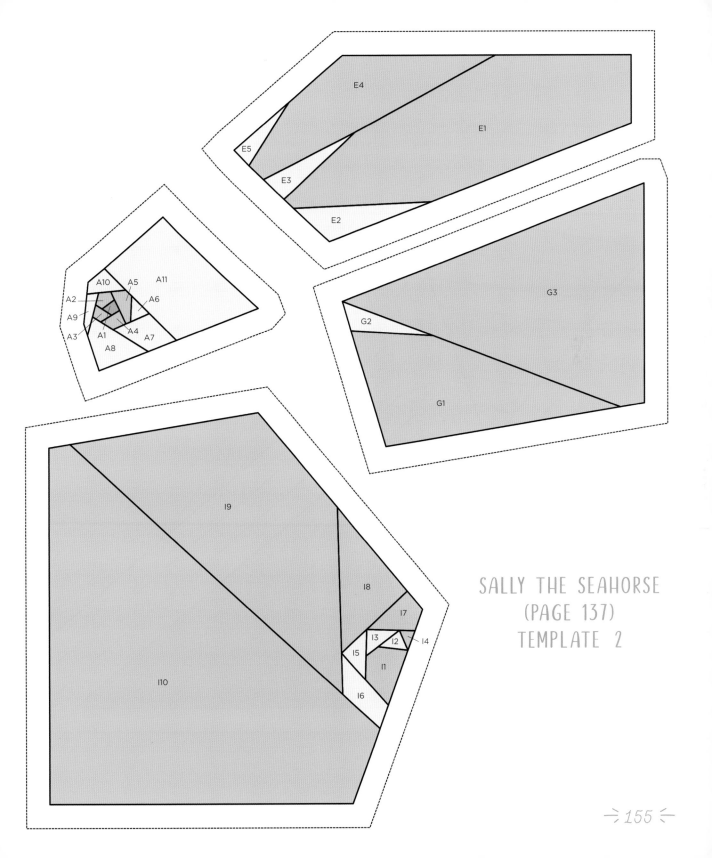

SALLY THE SEAHORSE
(PAGE 137)
TEMPLATE 2

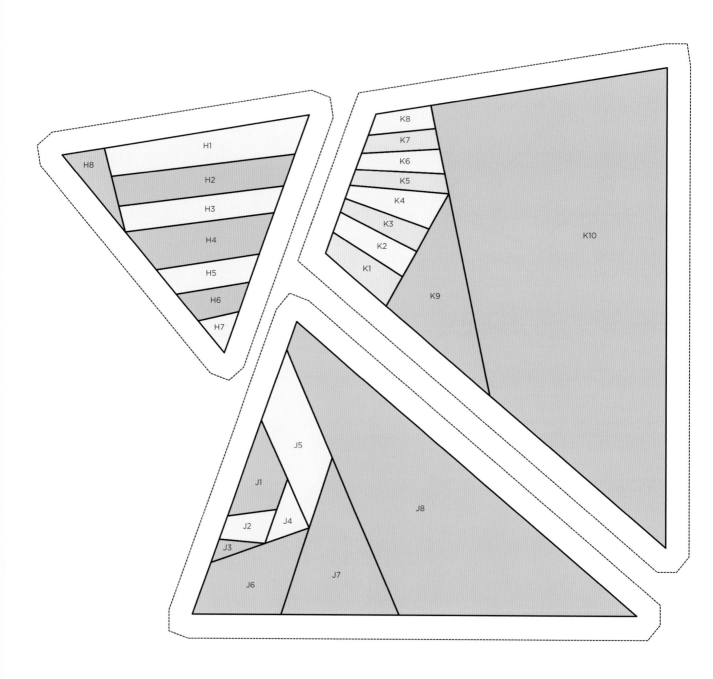

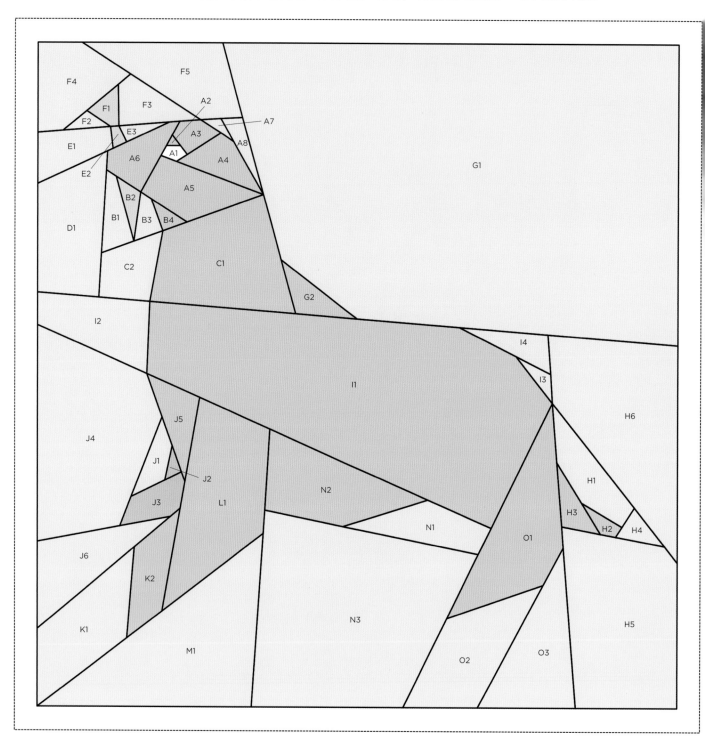

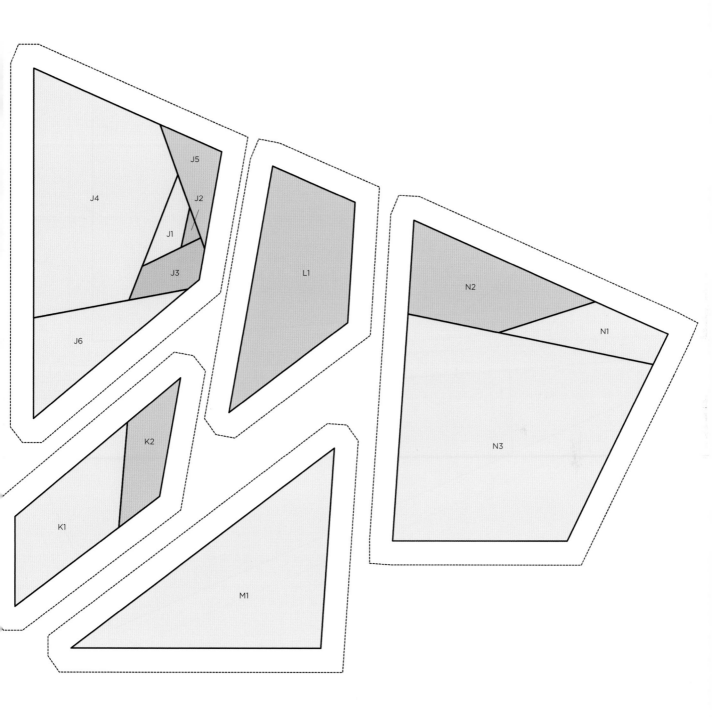

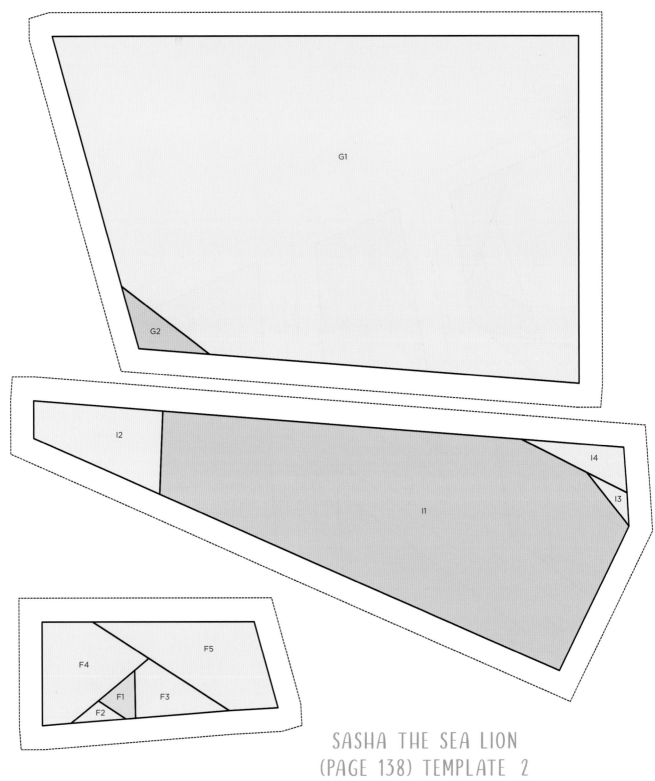

SASHA THE SEA LION
(PAGE 138) TEMPLATE 2

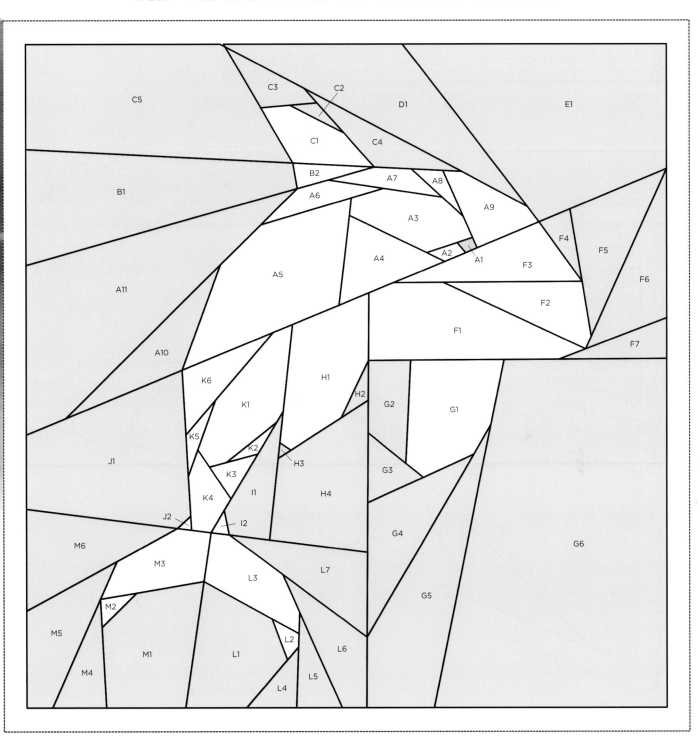

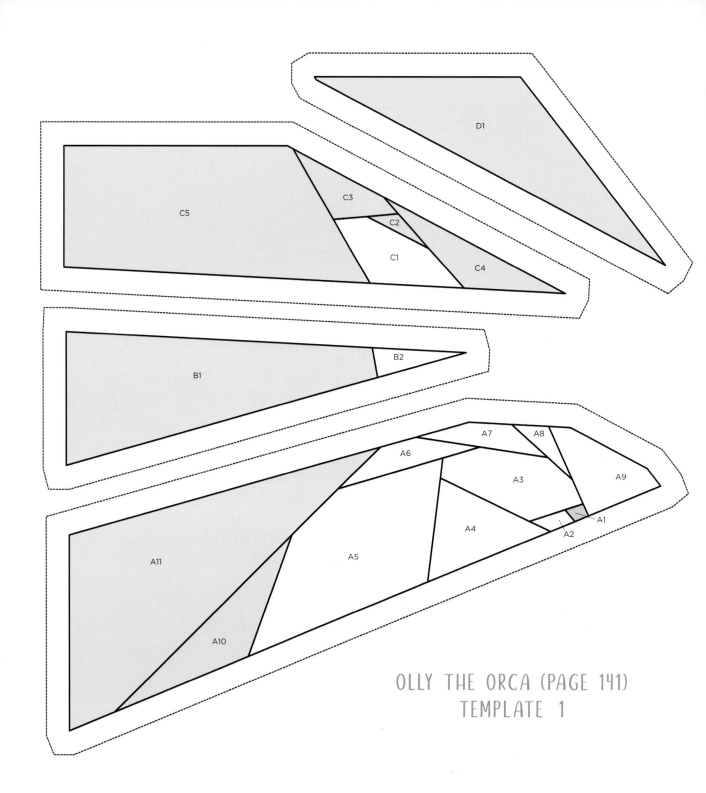

OLLY THE ORCA (PAGE 141)
TEMPLATE 1

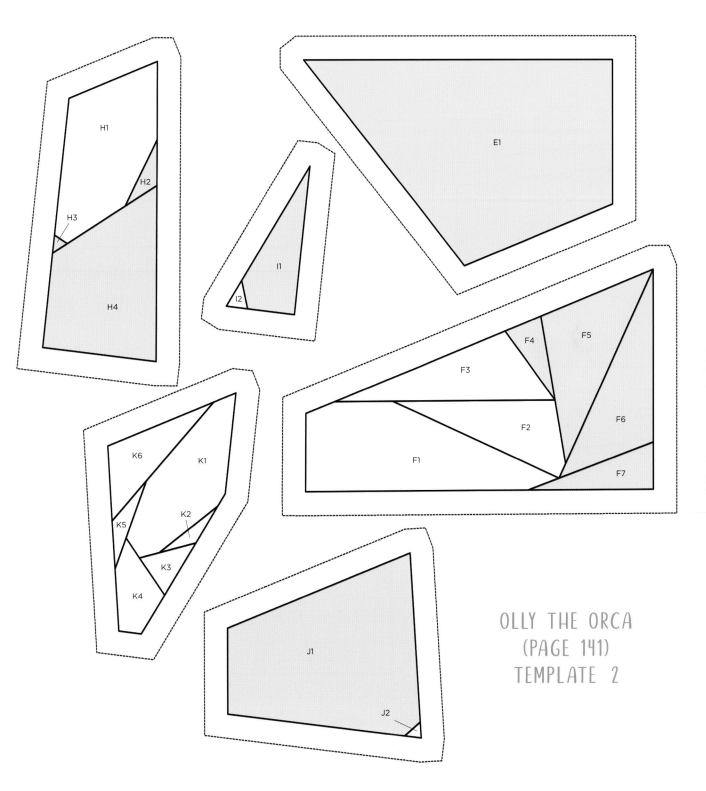

OLLY THE ORCA
(PAGE 141)
TEMPLATE 2

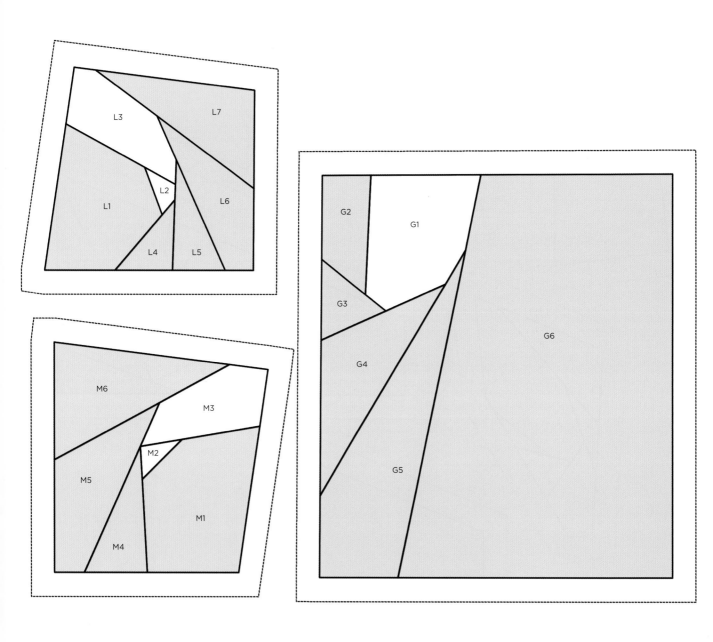

Acknowledgments

Writing a book was something I always dreamed about but never actually thought would happen, so this is a real dream come true.

I'd like to say a huge thank you to my husband, Chris, and my three children, Jonas, Sophie and Eva, for their support in this adventure. Without their love and understanding, this would not have been possible.

Thank you, Jonas, for taking all the photos in this book and for providing feedback and lots of inspiration. I really appreciate it.

A special thank you to my mom, Johanna, who taught me crafts, and how to sew in particular, and who planted that first seed of "love for crafts" early on.

Thank you to my late father, Karl, from whom I inherited my artistic streak and who inspired me to pursue a creative career. I miss you tons.

And finally a big thank you to the team at Page Street Publishing; you were amazing at making my vision of this book come to life. Especially Caitlin Dow and Sarah Monroe for always listening to my ideas and incorporating them into a wonderful book.

About the Author

Ingrid Alteneder has been sewing since she was a child. She has worked with fabrics all of her adult life, including as a fashion buyer and CEO of her own fashion label. After leaving the fashion industry, she continued to work with fabrics, first as a sewing and crafts teacher and then as a quilt block designer. Quilting has been her hobby since high school and foundation paper piecing is the icing on the cake. Her love for bright colors and her eye for unique fabric combinations make her designs stand out. Her work was featured in several quilting industry magazines, such as *Love Patchwork & Quilting Magazine*, *Patchwork* magazine (Germany) and others, as well as at numerous quilt stores in Europe. Check out her website, www.joejuneandmae.de, for more patterns, tutorials and inspiration.

INSTAGRAM
@joejuneandmae

PINTEREST
JoeJuneandMae

FACEBOOK
Joe June and Mae

ETSY
etsy.com/shop/joejuneandmae

Index